CODE, BYTES, ALGORITHMS, AND INNOVATION:
SOFTWARE & ENGINEERING

Tobi Makinde

Copyright © 2023 All rights reserved. Tobi Makinde

Code, Bytes, Algorithms, And Innovation: Software & Engineering

No part of this book may be reproduced or transmitted in any form or by any means, electronic or mechanical, including photocopying, recording, or by any information storage and retrieval system, without permission in writing from the Copyright owner.

Any information is to be used for educational and information purposes only. It should never be substituted for financial advice.

The author or publisher does not in any way endorse any commercial products or services linked from other websites to this book.

Globally Available

Published by:
Emphaloz Publishing House
www.emphaloz.com
publish@emphaloz.com

ISBN: 978-7-5200-5752-3

A catalogue record of this book will be available from the National Library of Nigeria.

TABLE OF CONTENTS

TABLE OF CONTENTS III
PREFACE IV
INTRODUCTION VIII

CHAPTER 1: THE EVOLUTION OF SOFTWARE ENGINEERING 1
CHAPTER 2: UNDERSTANDING PROGRAMMING LANGUAGES 7
CHAPTER 3: THE ART OF ALGORITHM DESIGN 13
CHAPTER 4: DATA STRUCTURES AND THEIR IMPORTANCE 19
CHAPTER 5: SOFTWARE DEVELOPMENT METHODOLOGIES 24
CHAPTER 6: SOFTWARE TESTING AND QUALITY ASSURANCE 32
CHAPTER 7: SOFTWARE MAINTENANCE AND EVOLUTION 38
CHAPTER 8: THE ROLE OF PROJECT MANAGEMENT IN SOFTWARE ENGINEERING 44
CHAPTER 9: COLLABORATION IN SOFTWARE ENGINEERING 51
CHAPTER 10: SOFTWARE SECURITY AND ETHICAL HACKING 57
CHAPTER 11: THE FUTURE OF SOFTWARE ENGINEERING 64
CHAPTER 12: THE INTERSECTION OF SOFTWARE AND HARDWARE 70
CHAPTER 13: OPEN-SOURCE SOFTWARE AND COMMUNITY DEVELOPMENT 77
CHAPTER 14: THE BUSINESS OF SOFTWARE ENGINEERING 82
CHAPTER 15: BUILDING A CAREER IN SOFTWARE ENGINEERING 88
CHAPTER 16: THE IMPACT OF EMERGING TECHNOLOGIES ON SOFTWARE ENGINEERING 93
CHAPTER 17: FUTURE TRENDS IN SOFTWARE ENGINEERING 98

PREFACE

Welcome to "Code, Bytes, Algorithms, and Innovation: Software & Engineer." In an era where technology is the backbone of almost every aspect of our lives, the role of software engineering has never been more critical. As we stand on the brink of unprecedented technological advancements, understanding the intricacies of software engineering becomes paramount. This book, "Code, Bytes, Algorithms, and Innovation: Software & Engineer," is a comprehensive exploration of the fundamental principles, methodologies, and emerging trends in software engineering. It aims to provide both novice and experienced software engineers with a deep understanding of the field, equipping them with the knowledge and skills needed to navigate the complexities of modern software development.

The journey of writing this book has been both challenging and rewarding. It involved extensive research, numerous revisions, and countless hours of contemplation to ensure that the content is both accurate and relevant. The goal was to create a resource that is not only informative but also engaging, providing readers with practical insights and real-world applications of software engineering concepts. Each chapter has been meticulously crafted to cover different aspects of software engineering, from the evolution of programming languages and the art of algorithm design to the latest advancements in artificial intelligence and quantum computing.

One of the key motivations behind this book is the desire to demystify software engineering for those who may find it intimidating. The field can often seem daunting, with its complex terminology, rapid technological changes, and the sheer breadth of knowledge required. By breaking down these complexities into manageable sections and explaining concepts in a clear and accessible manner, this book aims to make software engineering more approachable and less overwhelming.

Another driving force behind this book is the recognition of the importance of continuous learning in the field of software engineering. Technology evolves at a rapid pace, and staying current with the latest developments is crucial for success. This book encourages a mindset of lifelong learning, emphasizing the need for software engineers to continually update their skills and knowledge. Whether through online courses, certifications, professional communities, or open-source contributions, the path to becoming a proficient software engineer is one of ongoing education and adaptation.

The collaborative nature of software engineering is also a central theme of this book. The field thrives on teamwork, communication, and the sharing of knowledge. Open-source software and community-driven development have revolutionized the way we build software, fostering innovation and creating robust, reliable solutions. This book highlights the significance of collaboration, providing insights into effective team management, project management methodologies, and the principles of open-source software development.

In addition to technical skills, the book emphasizes the importance of soft skills in software engineering. Effective communication, problem-solving, and adaptability are just as crucial as technical proficiency. These skills enable software engineers to work effectively in diverse teams, navigate complex projects, and deliver high-quality software that meets user needs. By incorporating discussions on soft skills and professional development, this book aims to provide a holistic view of what it takes to succeed in the field of software engineering.

This book would not have been possible without the support and contributions of many individuals. I am deeply grateful to the experts, colleagues, and friends who shared their insights, provided feedback, and offered encouragement throughout this journey. Their contributions have enriched the content and ensured that they reflect the latest trends and best practices in software engineering.

I also want to express my gratitude to the readers who inspire the creation of such works. Your passion for learning and your dedication to the field of software engineering motivate authors like me to continue exploring, researching, and sharing knowledge. It is my hope that this book will serve as a valuable resource on your journey, helping you to navigate the ever-evolving landscape of software engineering and achieve your professional goals.

In conclusion, "Code, Bytes, Algorithms, and Innovation: Software & Engineer" is a labor of love, born out of a deep respect for the field of software engineering and a desire to contribute to its growth. It is a comprehensive guide that covers a wide range of topics, from the foundational principles to the cutting-edge technologies shaping the future of software engineering. Whether you are a student, a seasoned professional, or someone with a keen interest in technology, I hope that this book will provide you with valuable insights, practical knowledge, and the inspiration to continue learning and innovating in the field of software engineering.

INTRODUCTION

Software engineering is the art and science of designing, developing, and maintaining software systems. It is a discipline that combines technical knowledge, problem-solving skills, and creativity to build software that meets user needs and performs reliably under various conditions. As the world becomes increasingly digital, the demand for skilled software engineers continues to grow, making it a dynamic and rewarding field with endless possibilities.

The field of software engineering has evolved significantly over the past few decades. From the early days of programming with punch cards and assembly language to the modern era of cloud computing, artificial intelligence, and quantum computing, software engineering has continually adapted to new technologies and methodologies. This evolution has been driven by the need to create more efficient, reliable, and scalable software systems that can handle the complexities of today's digital landscape.

At its core, software engineering is about solving problems. Whether it is developing a mobile application that helps people manage their health, creating software that powers autonomous vehicles, or building systems that process vast amounts of data in real-time, software engineers use their skills and knowledge to address a wide range of challenges. This problem-solving aspect is what makes software engineering both challenging and exciting, as it requires a combination of analytical thinking, creativity, and technical expertise.

One of the fundamental principles of software engineering is the importance of design. Good software design involves creating a blueprint that guides the development process, ensuring that the final product is robust, maintainable, and scalable. Design principles such as modularity, abstraction, and encapsulation help manage the complexity of software systems, making them easier to understand, modify, and extend. Design patterns, which provide reusable solutions to common problems, play a crucial role in creating effective software architectures.

Another key aspect of software engineering is the use of methodologies and frameworks to guide the development process. Methodologies such as Agile, Scrum, and DevOps emphasize collaboration, flexibility, and continuous improvement, enabling teams to deliver high-quality software quickly and efficiently. These methodologies promote iterative development, regular feedback, and adaptive planning, allowing software engineers to respond to changing requirements and deliver value to users more effectively.

Testing and quality assurance are also critical components of software engineering. Ensuring that software performs as expected and is free from defects is essential for delivering reliable and high-quality products. Various testing techniques, including unit testing, integration testing, and acceptance testing, help identify and address issues early in the development process. Automated testing tools and frameworks further enhance the efficiency and effectiveness of testing, enabling continuous integration and delivery.

The role of software engineers extends beyond technical skills. Effective communication, teamwork, and project management are vital for successful software development. Software engineers must be able to collaborate with colleagues, stakeholders, and users, conveying complex technical concepts in a clear and understandable manner. They must also be able to manage their time, prioritize tasks, and work efficiently in a fast-paced and often unpredictable environment.

In recent years, several emerging technologies have begun to reshape the field of software engineering. Artificial intelligence and machine learning are enabling the development of intelligent systems that can learn and adapt over time. Blockchain technology is providing new ways to secure and verify transactions, creating opportunities for innovation in finance, supply chain, and beyond. Quantum computing promises to revolutionize the way we solve complex problems, offering unprecedented computational power for tasks such as cryptography, optimization, and simulation.

As we look to the future, the field of software engineering will continue to evolve, driven by advancements in technology and changes in the way we work and live. The rise of remote work, the increasing importance of cybersecurity, and the growing emphasis on data privacy are just a few of the trends that will shape the future of software engineering. Software engineers must be adaptable, continuously updating their skills and knowledge to stay ahead of these changes and seize new opportunities.

In writing "Code, Bytes, Algorithms, and Innovation: Software & Engineer," my goal is to provide a comprehensive and accessible guide to the field of software engineering. This book covers a wide range of topics, from the foundational principles and methodologies to the latest trends and technologies shaping the future of software development. Each chapter delves into a specific aspect of software engineering, providing detailed explanations, practical examples, and insights from industry experts.

Whether you are a student just beginning your journey in software engineering, a professional looking to expand your knowledge and skills, or someone with a keen interest in technology, I hope that this book will serve as a valuable resource. It is designed to be both informative and engaging, offering a blend of theory and practice that will help you understand the complexities of software engineering and apply this knowledge to real-world problems.

In conclusion, software engineering is a dynamic and ever-evolving field that offers endless opportunities for innovation and impact. By understanding the principles, methodologies, and emerging trends, you can navigate the complexities of this field and contribute to the creation of software that makes a difference in the world. "Code, Bytes, Algorithms, and Innovation: Software & Engineer" is your guide to this exciting journey, providing the knowledge and inspiration you need to succeed in the world of software engineering.

CHAPTER 1
The Evolution of Software Engineering

Software engineering has come a long way since its inception, evolving through various phases and technological advancements to become the sophisticated field it is today. The concept of software engineering began to take shape in the 1960s. During this period, software development was primarily an ad-hoc process, often resulting in projects that were over budget, behind schedule, and riddled with bugs. The term "software engineering" was first introduced at the 1968 NATO Software Engineering Conference in Garmisch, Germany, where experts gathered to address the growing "software crisis." The crisis referred to the difficulties in developing reliable and efficient software systems on time and within budget. The Garmisch conference highlighted the need for systematic approaches and methodologies to tackle the complexities of software development. The participants recognized that developing software was not merely about coding but required engineering principles, planning, and management. This realization marked the beginning of software engineering as a discipline.

The 1970s witnessed the development of early methodologies aimed at improving software development processes. One of the most significant advancements during this era was the introduction of structured programming. Pioneered by computer scientists like Edger Dijkstra, structured programming emphasized the use of clear, hierarchical control structures, such as loops and conditionals, to create more readable and maintainable code. This approach aimed to reduce the complexity and increase the reliability of software. The Waterfall model, introduced by Winston Royce in 1970, became one of the first formalized software development methodologies. The Waterfall model followed a linear, sequential approach, with distinct phases such as requirements gathering, design, implementation, testing, and maintenance. While the Waterfall model provided a structured framework, its rigidity and lack of flexibility made it challenging to accommodate changes once a phase was completed.

The 1980s saw the emergence of object-oriented programming (OOP), a paradigm that revolutionized software development. OOP introduced the concept of encapsulating data and behavior into objects, which could be reused and extended to create more modular and scalable systems. Programming languages like Smalltalk, C++, and later Java and Python, popularized the object-oriented approach. OOP facilitated the development of complex software systems by promoting code reuse, modularity, and abstraction. The principles of inheritance, polymorphism, and encapsulation provided a robust framework for designing software that could evolve and adapt to changing requirements. This paradigm shift laid the foundation for modern software engineering practices.

The late 1990s and early 2000s marked a significant shift in software development methodologies with the rise of Agile methodologies. Agile emerged as a response to the limitations of traditional, linear approaches like the Waterfall model. Agile methodologies, such as Scrum, Kanban, and Extreme Programming (XP), emphasized iterative development, customer collaboration, and flexibility. The Agile Manifesto, published in 2001, outlined key principles for Agile development, prioritizing individuals and interactions, working software, customer collaboration, and responding to change. Agile methodologies promoted the idea of delivering small, incremental improvements through short development cycles, known as sprints. This approach allowed teams to gather feedback early and often, adapt to changing requirements, and deliver value to customers more quickly.

The early 2000s also saw the rise of open-source software and community-driven development. Open-source projects, such as the Linux operating system, Apache web server, and Mozilla Firefox browser, demonstrated the power of collaborative development. Developers from around the world could contribute to these projects, sharing their code, knowledge, and expertise. The open-source movement challenged traditional notions of software development and distribution, promoting transparency, collaboration, and the democratization of technology. Open-source licenses, such as the GNU General Public License (GPL) and the MIT License, provided legal frameworks that allowed developers to use, modify, and distribute software freely. The success of open-source projects highlighted the importance of community involvement and paved the way for new models of software development.

In the 2010s, the DevOps movement emerged, further transforming software engineering practices. DevOps, a portmanteau of "development" and "operations," emphasized collaboration and integration between development and operations teams. The goal of DevOps was to streamline the software delivery process, improve efficiency, and reduce the time it took to bring new features to market. Continuous Integration (CI) and Continuous Delivery (CD) became core practices within the DevOps framework. CI involved automatically integrating code changes from multiple contributors into a shared repository, running automated tests to detect integration issues early. CD extended this concept by automating the deployment of tested and validated code to production environments. These practices enabled teams to deliver high-quality software quickly and reliably. DevOps also introduced the concept of "Infrastructure as Code" (IaC), which involved managing and provisioning infrastructure using code and automation tools. This approach allowed for consistent and repeatable infrastructure deployments, reducing the risk of configuration drift and improving scalability.

As we move into the 2020s, artificial intelligence (AI) and machine learning (ML) are playing an increasingly important role in software engineering. AI and ML technologies are being integrated into various stages of the software development lifecycle, from code generation and bug detection to performance optimization and user experience enhancement. AI-driven tools and platforms, such as GitHub Copilot and DeepCode, are automating code suggestions, identifying vulnerabilities, and recommending optimizations. Machine learning models can analyze vast amounts of data to predict and prevent software failures, enabling more proactive and intelligent development practices. Moreover, AI and ML are driving advancements in areas such as natural language processing (NLP) and computer vision, opening up new possibilities for software applications. For example, NLP can be used to improve code documentation, generate summaries of complex codebases, and facilitate communication between developers and stakeholders.

The evolution of software engineering is an ongoing journey, shaped by continuous innovation and adaptation. Emerging technologies, such as blockchain, quantum computing, and edge computing, are poised to drive the next wave of advancements in the field. Blockchain technology, with its decentralized and secure nature, has the potential to revolutionize industries such as finance, supply chain, and healthcare. Quantum computing, leveraging the principles of quantum mechanics, promises to solve complex problems that are currently intractable for classical computers. Edge computing, which involves processing data closer to the source, is reshaping the way software is deployed and managed, enabling more efficient and responsive systems. The future of software engineering will also be influenced by increasing emphasis on data privacy and security, driven by regulations such as the General Data Protection Regulation (GDPR) and the California Consumer Privacy Act (CCPA). Software engineers must prioritize privacy and security in their designs, employing techniques such as differential privacy, homomorphic encryption, and secure multi-party computation. In conclusion, the evolution of software engineering is a testament to the field's adaptability and resilience. From its early beginnings in the 1960s to the present day, software engineering has undergone significant transformations, driven by technological advancements, methodological innovations, and community collaboration. As we look to the future, the field will continue to evolve, embracing new technologies and practices that will shape the way we develop, deploy, and maintain software.

CHAPTER 2
Understanding Programming Languages

Programming languages are the foundation of software engineering. They provide the means for developers to communicate with computers and create software that powers our modern world. The history of programming languages dates to the mid-20th century, with the development of the first electronic computers. Early programming languages were often specific to the hardware they ran on and were written in machine code or assembly language. These low-level languages provided direct control over the hardware but were challenging to write, read, and maintain. The need for more abstract and human-readable programming languages led to the development of high-level languages. In the late 1950s, FORTRAN (FORmula TRANslation) was introduced by IBM for scientific and engineering applications. FORTRAN allowed programmers to write code using mathematical notation, making it easier to solve complex computational problems. Around the same time, COBOL (COmmon Business-Oriented Language) was developed for business data processing.

COBOL's syntax was designed to be readable and understandable by non-programmers, making it suitable for applications such as payroll and inventory management. These early high-level languages marked the beginning of a shift towards more accessible and versatile programming tools.

The 1960s and 1970s saw the emergence of structured programming, a paradigm that emphasized the use of clear and hierarchical control structures. This approach aimed to improve readability, maintainability, and reliability. The introduction of languages like ALGOL (ALGOrithmic Language), Pascal, and C played a significant role in popularizing structured programming. ALGOL, developed in the late 1950s and early 1960s, introduced many concepts that became fundamental to programming languages, such as block structure, nested functions, and recursive procedures. Pascal, designed by Niklaus Wirth in the late 1960s, further refined these ideas and became a popular language for teaching programming and developing early software applications. C, developed by Dennis Ritchie at Bell Labs in the early 1970s, combined the efficiency of low-level programming with the abstraction of high-level languages. C's versatility and performance made it a preferred choice for system programming, operating systems, and embedded systems. The language's influence is still evident today, with many modern languages, such as C++, C#, and Java, drawing inspiration from C.

The 1980s marked a significant shift in programming paradigms with the rise of object-oriented programming (OOP). OOP introduced the concept of encapsulating data and behavior into objects, which could be reused and extended to create more modular and scalable systems. Languages like Smalltalk, C++, and later Java and Python, popularized the object-oriented approach. Smalltalk, developed in the 1970s at Xerox PARC, was one of the earliest pure object-oriented languages. It emphasized message passing between objects and dynamic binding, laying the groundwork for many OOP principles. C++, developed by Bjarne Stroustrup in the early 1980s, extended the C language with object-oriented features, making it a powerful tool for system and application development. Java, introduced by Sun Microsystems in the mid-1990s, further popularized OOP with its "write once, run anywhere" philosophy. Java's platform independence, achieved through the Java Virtual Machine (JVM), allowed developers to write code that could run on any device with a JVM, fostering the growth of web and enterprise applications.

The 1990s and 2000s saw the rise of scripting languages, which were designed for rapid development and ease of use. Scripting languages like Perl, Python, and Ruby became popular for tasks such as web development, system administration, and automation. Perl, developed by Larry Wall in the late 1980s, was initially created for text processing and system administration tasks. Its flexibility and powerful regular expression capabilities made it a favorite among system administrators and web developers. Python, designed by Guido van Rossum in the late 1980s and early 1990s, emphasized readability and simplicity, making it accessible to beginners and experienced developers alike. Ruby, created by Yukihiro "Matz" Matsumoto in the mid-1990s, combined the best features of Perl, Smalltalk, and Lisp to create a language that was both powerful and elegant. Ruby on Rails, a web application framework written in Ruby, revolutionized web development by promoting convention over configuration and enabling rapid development of web applications.

Functional programming, a paradigm that treats computation as the evaluation of mathematical functions, has been around since the early days of programming languages. However, it gained renewed interest and popularity in the 2000s and 2010s as developers sought new ways to handle the complexities of modern software development. Languages like Lisp and Scheme, developed in the 1950s and 1970s respectively, were early examples of functional programming languages. They introduced concepts such as first-class functions, recursion, and immutability, which are central to functional programming. The resurgence of functional programming was driven by languages like Haskell, Erlang, and Scala. Haskell, a purely functional language developed in the late 1980s and 1990s, emphasized lazy evaluation, type safety, and immutability. Erlang, developed by Ericsson in the 1980s, was designed for concurrent and distributed systems, making it ideal for telecommunications and real-time applications. Scala, a language that seamlessly integrates object-oriented and functional programming, gained popularity in the 2000s for its ability to run on the JVM and its support for modern programming paradigms. The adoption of functional programming concepts in mainstream languages like JavaScript, C#, and Python further underscored the paradigm's relevance and influence.

As we move into the 2020s, several trends are shaping the future of programming languages. One significant trend is the rise of domain-specific languages (DSLs), which are tailored to specific application domains. DSLs provide concise and expressive syntax for tasks such as data analysis, machine learning, and configuration management. Examples include SQL for database queries, R for statistical computing, and TensorFlow for machine learning. Another trend is the increasing emphasis on type safety and correctness. Modern languages like Rust, developed by Mozilla, and TypeScript, a superset of JavaScript, prioritize type safety and compile-time checks to catch errors early and improve code reliability. Rust, in particular, has gained attention for its focus on memory safety and concurrency, making it suitable for system programming and performance-critical applications. The rise of multicore processors and parallel computing has also driven the adoption of concurrent and parallel programming paradigms. Languages like Go, developed by Google, and Elixir, built on the Erlang VM, provide abstractions for writing concurrent and distributed systems. These languages enable developers to harness the full potential of modern hardware and build scalable and efficient software. The integration of artificial intelligence and machine learning into programming languages is another emerging trend. Languages like Julia, designed for high-performance numerical computing, and Python, with its extensive machine learning libraries, are becoming the go-to choices for AI and data science applications. These languages provide the tools and frameworks needed to develop, train, and deploy machine learning models. In conclusion, the evolution of programming languages is a testament to the field's adaptability and innovation. From the early days of machine code and assembly language to the modern era of high-level, domain-specific, and functional languages, programming languages have continuously evolved to meet the needs of developers and the challenges of software development. As new technologies and paradigms emerge, programming languages will continue to evolve, enabling developers to create more powerful, efficient, and reliable software.

CHAPTER 3
The Art of Algorithm Design

Algorithm design is a cornerstone of software engineering, providing the foundation for solving complex problems and building efficient software systems. Algorithms are step-by-step procedures for solving problems and performing tasks. They are the building blocks of software, enabling computers to process data, make decisions, and execute commands. The design and analysis of algorithms are critical for developing software that is efficient, reliable, and scalable. The significance of algorithms can be traced back to ancient times, with the development of early mathematical techniques and procedures. The word "algorithm" itself is derived from the name of the Persian mathematician Al-Khwarizmi, whose works on arithmetic and algebra laid the groundwork for modern algorithmic thinking. In the context of software engineering, algorithms are essential for a wide range of applications, from sorting and searching data to optimizing network traffic and securing communication. The efficiency of an algorithm can have a profound impact on the performance and scalability of software systems. Efficient algorithms enable software to process large volumes of data quickly, respond to user inputs in real-time, and operate within resource constraints.

Algorithm design involves several fundamental concepts and techniques, each of which plays a crucial role in developing effective solutions. Clearly defining the problem to be solved is the first step in algorithm design. This involves understanding the input, output, constraints, and requirements of the problem. A well-defined problem provides a clear framework for developing and evaluating potential solutions. Abstraction involves simplifying a problem by focusing on its essential features and ignoring irrelevant details. This allows for the creation of general and reusable solutions. For example, sorting algorithms abstract the problem of arranging items in a specific order, allowing them to be applied to various types of data. Analyzing an algorithm involves evaluating its efficiency in terms of time and space complexity. Time complexity measures the number of operations an algorithm performs relative to the input size, while space complexity measures the amount of memory it uses. Big O notation is commonly used to express the complexity of an algorithm, providing a way to compare different algorithms and assess their scalability. Several design techniques are used to develop algorithms, each suited to different types of problems. Divide and Conquer involves breaking a problem into smaller subproblems, solving each subproblem independently, and combining the solutions to solve the original problem. Examples include merge sort and quicksort. Dynamic Programming is used to solve problems with overlapping subproblems and optimal substructure. It involves storing the results of subproblems to avoid redundant computations. Examples include the Fibonacci sequence and the knapsack problem. Greedy Algorithms make locally optimal choices at each step, aiming to find a global optimum. They are often used for optimization problems, such as finding the shortest path in a graph or constructing a minimum spanning tree. Examples include Dijkstra's algorithm and Kruskal's algorithm. Backtracking is used to solve constraint satisfaction problems by exploring possible solutions and abandoning paths that do not satisfy the constraints. Examples include the N-Queens problem and the knapsack problem. Ensuring the correctness of an algorithm involves proving that it produces the correct output for all possible inputs. This can be achieved through formal methods, such as mathematical induction, as well as empirical testing with a variety of test cases. Testing helps identify edge cases and potential errors, ensuring the reliability of the algorithm.

The history of algorithm design is marked by several significant milestones and contributions from mathematicians, computer scientists, and engineers. One of the earliest known algorithms, Euclid's algorithm, was developed around 300 BCE for finding the greatest common divisor (GCD) of two numbers. This algorithm exemplifies the principles of recursion and iteration, which are fundamental to many modern algorithms. In the 1930s, Alan Turing introduced the concept of the Turing machine, a theoretical model of computation that could simulate any algorithm. Turing's work laid the foundation for the field of computer science and formalized the concept of algorithmic computation. The development of efficient sorting algorithms, such as merge sort, quicksort, and heapsort, was a significant milestone in algorithm design. These algorithms demonstrated the power of divide-and-conquer techniques and established benchmarks for algorithmic efficiency. The study of graph algorithms, including Dijkstra's algorithm for shortest paths and Prim's and Kruskal's algorithms for minimum spanning trees, has had a profound impact on fields such as network design, transportation, and social networks. These algorithms provided efficient solutions to fundamental problems in graph theory and optimization. In the 1970s, Stephen Cook and Richard Karp introduced the concept of NP-completeness, a classification of problems for which no known efficient solutions exist. The theory of NP-completeness has guided research in computational complexity and helped identify the boundaries of algorithmic feasibility.

Algorithm design continues to be a vibrant and evolving field, with new applications and challenges emerging in various domains. Algorithms play a central role in data science and machine learning, enabling the analysis and interpretation of large datasets. Techniques such as clustering, classification, regression, and neural networks are built on foundational algorithms that process and learn from data. Cryptographic algorithms are essential for securing communication, protecting data, and ensuring privacy. Algorithms such as RSA, AES, and SHA are used to encrypt data, generate digital signatures, and verify integrity. The design of cryptographic algorithms requires a deep understanding of mathematics, number theory, and computational complexity. Algorithm design is crucial for solving problems in bioinformatics, such as DNA sequencing, protein folding, and phylogenetic analysis. Algorithms are used to compare genetic sequences, predict molecular structures, and identify evolutionary relationships, contributing to advances in biology and medicine. Algorithms are the backbone of robotics and autonomous systems, enabling tasks such as path planning, localization, and object recognition. Algorithms such as A*, SLAM (Simultaneous Localization and Mapping), and computer vision techniques empower robots to navigate, perceive, and interact with their environments. Algorithmic trading, risk assessment, and portfolio optimization rely on sophisticated algorithms to analyze market data, identify trends, and make investment decisions. These algorithms process large volumes of financial data in real-time, providing insights and strategies for maximizing returns and managing risk.

The future of algorithm design is shaped by ongoing research, technological advancements, and emerging challenges. Quantum computing represents a significant frontier in algorithm design. Quantum algorithms, such as Shor's algorithm for factoring and Grover's algorithm for search, promise to solve certain types of problems exponentially faster than classical algorithms. The development of quantum algorithms requires rethinking traditional approaches and exploring the unique properties of quantum mechanics. The integration of artificial intelligence and machine learning with algorithm design is another exciting area of research. AI-driven approaches, such as reinforcement learning and genetic algorithms, are being used to develop adaptive and self-optimizing algorithms. These techniques enable algorithms to learn from data, adapt to changing conditions, and improve their performance over time. In conclusion, algorithm design is a fundamental and dynamic field that underpins the development of efficient and effective software systems. From ancient mathematical techniques to modern applications in data science, cryptography, and robotics, algorithms continue to play a central role in solving complex problems and advancing technology. As new challenges and opportunities arise, the field of algorithm design will continue to evolve, driving innovation and shaping the future of software engineering.

CHAPTER 4
Data Structures and Their Importance

Data structures are the backbone of software engineering, providing the means to organize, store, and manage data efficiently. Data structures are fundamental components of software systems, enabling the efficient manipulation and retrieval of data. They provide the framework for organizing data in a way that supports specific operations, such as searching, sorting, and updating. The choice of data structure can have a significant impact on the performance and scalability of software applications. The importance of data structures lies in their ability to optimize algorithms and improve the efficiency of operations. For example, a well-chosen data structure can reduce the time complexity of an algorithm from linear to logarithmic, resulting in faster execution times and better resource utilization. Data structures also play a crucial role in memory management, helping to minimize memory usage and avoid fragmentation.

Several fundamental data structures form the building blocks of more complex structures and algorithms. Arrays are fixed-size collections of elements, stored in contiguous memory locations. They provide constant-time access to elements using an index, making them suitable for tasks that require frequent access to specific elements. However, their fixed size and lack of flexibility can be limitations in dynamic scenarios. Linked lists are dynamic data structures consisting of nodes, each containing a data element and a reference to the next node. Linked lists allow for efficient insertion and deletion of elements, but accessing elements requires traversing the list, resulting in linear time complexity. Stacks are linear data structures that follow the Last-In-First-Out (LIFO) principle. Elements are added and removed from the top of the stack. Stacks are commonly used in algorithms that require backtracking, such as depth-first search and expression evaluation. Queues are linear data structures that follow the First-In-First-Out (FIFO) principle. Elements are added at the rear and removed from the front. Queues are used in scenarios that require order preservation, such as task scheduling and breadth-first search. Trees are hierarchical data structures consisting of nodes connected by edges. Each node has a parent and zero or more children. Binary trees, where each node has at most two children, are commonly used for searching and sorting. Binary search trees (BSTs) provide efficient searching, insertion, and deletion operations. Heaps are specialized binary trees used to implement priority queues. They maintain a specific order property, such as the maximum or minimum element being at the root. Heaps are used in algorithms like heap sort and for managing resource allocation. Hash tables are data structures that provide constant-time average-case access to elements using a hash function. They store key-value pairs, allowing for efficient searching, insertion, and deletion. Hash tables are widely used in applications like caching, database indexing, and symbol tables. Graphs are data structures consisting of vertices (nodes) and edges (connections). They can represent relationships and dependencies between entities. Graphs are used in a variety of applications, including network design, social networks, and recommendation systems.

In addition to fundamental data structures, several advanced data structures provide specialized capabilities for specific applications. Balanced trees, such as AVL trees and Red-Black trees, maintain a balanced structure to ensure efficient operations. They provide logarithmic time complexity for searching, insertion, and deletion. Balanced trees are used in databases and file systems to maintain sorted data. Tries are tree-like data structures used to store strings or sequences. They provide efficient prefix-based searching and are used in applications like autocomplete, spell checking, and IP routing. Bloom filters are probabilistic data structures used to test whether an element is a member of a set. They provide constant-time membership checks with a configurable false-positive rate. Bloom filters are used in network security, database indexing, and web caching. Segment trees are used for answering range queries efficiently, such as finding the minimum or maximum value in a range. They are used in applications like computational geometry, range queries, and interval problems. Suffix trees are specialized data structures used for string processing tasks, such as substring search and pattern matching. They provide linear-time construction and search operations. Suffix trees are used in bioinformatics, text indexing, and data compression.

Data structures are integral to the design and implementation of software systems, enabling efficient data management and processing. Data structures are used to organize and index data in databases, enabling efficient querying and retrieval. B-trees and hash tables are commonly used for indexing and managing database records. Operating systems use data structures to manage processes, memory, and file systems. Linked lists and queues are used for scheduling processes, while trees and hash tables are used for managing file systems and memory allocation. Data structures are used to manage network routing, packet forwarding, and data transmission. Graphs are used to represent network topologies, while queues and buffers manage data flow and congestion. Data structures are used to manage web content, handle user requests, and optimize performance. Tries and hash tables are used for URL routing and caching, while trees and graphs manage website navigation and recommendations. Data structures are used to store and process large datasets, train models, and make predictions. Matrices and tensors are used for numerical computations, while trees and graphs represent decision boundaries and feature relationships. Data structures are used to manage game states, render graphics, and handle user input. Arrays and matrices represent game boards, while trees and graphs manage game logic and pathfinding.

Selecting the appropriate data structure for a given problem is crucial for achieving optimal performance and efficiency. Analyzing the problem, understanding the requirements, constraints, and expected operations for the problem is the first step. Consider factors such as the size of the data, frequency of operations, and memory limitations. Evaluating trade-offs between different data structures in terms of time complexity, space complexity, and ease of implementation helps choose the data structure that best balances these factors for the specific use case. Leveraging existing data structure libraries and frameworks that provide optimized implementations saves development time and ensures reliable and efficient performance. Testing the chosen data structure with realistic datasets and scenarios, profiling the performance, and optimizing the implementation as needed to meet the desired requirements is essential. Anticipating future changes and scalability requirements, choosing data structures that can accommodate growth and adapt to evolving needs without significant rework is crucial. In conclusion, data structures are fundamental components of software engineering, enabling efficient data organization, management, and processing. From basic arrays and linked lists to advanced tries and segment trees, data structures provide the foundation for developing high-performance software systems. Understanding the principles, applications, and best practices of data structures is essential for any software engineer, as it empowers them to build efficient, scalable, and reliable software.

CHAPTER 5
Software Development Methodologies

Software development methodologies provide the frameworks and processes that guide the creation of software. These methodologies have evolved over time, each offering distinct approaches to handling the complexities of software development. This chapter explores the various software development methodologies, their principles, advantages, and challenges, and how they have shaped the field of software engineering.

The Waterfall model, one of the earliest and most traditional software development methodologies, was introduced by Winston Royce in 1970. This model follows a linear and sequential approach, with each phase of development flowing into the next. The phases typically include requirements gathering, design, implementation, testing, deployment, and maintenance. The Waterfall model's structured nature provides clear milestones and deliverables at each stage, making it easier to manage and document the progress of the project. However, its rigidity and lack of flexibility can be significant drawbacks. Once a phase is completed, it is challenging to go back and make changes, which can be problematic if requirements evolve or unforeseen issues arise. This model is best suited for projects with well-defined and stable requirements.

In response to the limitations of the Waterfall model, iterative and incremental development methodologies began to gain traction. These methodologies break the development process into smaller, more manageable iterations or increments. Each iteration involves a mini-cycle of requirements gathering, design, implementation, and testing, allowing for continuous feedback and adjustments. The Rational Unified Process (RUP), developed by Rational Software (now part of IBM), is a prominent example of an iterative and incremental methodology. RUP divides the development process into four phases: inception, elaboration, construction, and transition. Each phase consists of multiple iterations, enabling teams to refine and enhance the software incrementally. This approach provides greater flexibility and allows for the incorporation of changes based on feedback from users and stakeholders.

Agile methodologies, which emerged in the late 1990s and early 2000s, represent a significant shift in software development practices. The Agile Manifesto, published in 2001, outlines key principles for Agile development, emphasizing individuals and interactions, working software, customer collaboration, and responding to change. Agile methodologies prioritize flexibility, adaptability, and continuous delivery of value to customers. Scrum, one of the most widely adopted Agile frameworks, organizes work into time-boxed iterations called sprints, typically lasting two to four weeks. During each sprint, cross-functional teams work collaboratively to deliver a potentially shippable product increment. Scrum roles, such as the Product Owner, Scrum Master, and Development Team, ensure clear responsibilities and effective communication. Daily stand-up meetings, sprint planning, sprint review, and sprint retrospective meetings foster transparency, inspection, and adaptation. The iterative nature of Scrum allows for frequent feedback and continuous improvement, enabling teams to respond to changing requirements and priorities.

Kanban, another Agile framework, focuses on visualizing work, limiting work in progress (WIP), and optimizing flow. Originating from Lean manufacturing principles, Kanban uses a visual board to represent the workflow, with columns representing different stages of the process. Work items are represented by cards that move across the board as they progress through the stages. By limiting the number of work items in each stage, Kanban helps identify bottlenecks, reduce lead times, and improve overall efficiency. Kanban promotes a continuous flow of work and encourages teams to make incremental improvements. Unlike Scrum, Kanban does not prescribe specific roles or time-boxed iterations, making it more flexible and adaptable to different contexts.

Extreme Programming (XP) is another Agile methodology that emphasizes technical excellence and high-quality code. XP practices, such as pair programming, test-driven development

(TDD), continuous integration, and frequent releases, aim to improve software quality and responsiveness to changing requirements. Pair programming involves two developers working together at the same workstation, with one writing code and the other reviewing it. This collaborative approach enhances code quality, knowledge sharing, and problem-solving. Test-driven development requires writing automated tests before writing the code that fulfills the test. This practice ensures that the code meets the desired behavior and facilitates early detection of defects. Continuous integration involves frequently integrating code changes into a shared repository and automatically running tests to detect integration issues. XP also emphasizes close collaboration with customers, who provide continuous feedback and help define requirements through user stories.

Lean Software Development, inspired by Lean manufacturing principles, focuses on delivering value to customers and eliminating waste. Lean principles, such as value stream mapping, just-in-time delivery, and continuous improvement, guide the development process. Value stream mapping involves analyzing the flow of value through the development process and identifying areas for improvement. Just-in-time delivery ensures that work is done only when needed, reducing inventory and minimizing waste. Continuous improvement, or Kaizen, encourages teams to regularly reflect on their processes and make incremental improvements. Lean practices, such as limiting WIP, visualizing workflow, and fostering a culture of learning, aim to create a more efficient and effective development process.

Feature-Driven Development (FDD) is an Agile methodology that focuses on delivering tangible, working software features. FDD follows a five-step process: develop an overall model, build a feature list, plan by feature, design by feature, and build by feature. Each feature is a small, client-valued function that can be developed and delivered within a short time frame, typically two weeks or less. FDD emphasizes the importance of accurate modeling, regular builds, and inspections to ensure the quality and completeness of features. By delivering features incrementally, FDD provides continuous value to customers and allows for flexible adaptation to changing requirements.

The Spiral model, introduced by Barry Boehm in the 1980s, combines elements of iterative and Waterfall models with a focus on risk management. The Spiral model involves repeated cycles, or spirals, each consisting of four phases: planning, risk analysis, engineering, and evaluation. During each cycle, the project team identifies and mitigates risks, develops and tests prototypes, and evaluates the results. The Spiral model allows for early identification and resolution of risks, making it suitable for large and complex projects with high levels of uncertainty. By incorporating feedback and lessons learned from each cycle, the Spiral model enables continuous refinement and improvement of the software.

DevOps, a cultural and technical movement that emerged in the 2010s, emphasizes collaboration, automation, and continuous delivery. DevOps aims to break down the traditional silos between development and operations teams, fostering a unified approach to delivering high-quality software quickly and reliably. DevOps practices, such as continuous integration, continuous delivery (CI/CD), infrastructure as code (IaC), and automated testing, streamline the development and deployment process. Continuous integration involves automatically integrating code changes into a shared repository and running automated tests to detect integration issues early. Continuous delivery extends CI by automating the deployment of tested and validated code to production environments. Infrastructure as code involves managing and provisioning infrastructure using code and automation tools, allowing for consistent and repeatable deployments. Automated testing ensures that code changes do not introduce new defects and helps maintain the quality and stability of the software. DevOps also emphasizes monitoring and feedback loops to continuously improve processes and address issues proactively.

The selection of an appropriate software development methodology depends on various factors, including the nature of the project, team size, organizational culture, and customer requirements. Each methodology has its strengths and challenges, and there is no one-size-fits-all solution. In many cases, organizations adopt a hybrid approach, combining elements from multiple methodologies to create a tailored process that best fits their needs.

One of the key benefits of Agile methodologies is their ability to accommodate changing requirements and deliver value to customers more quickly. The iterative and incremental nature of

Agile allows for continuous feedback and adaptation, reducing the risk of building software that does not meet user needs. Agile methodologies also promote collaboration and communication, fostering a culture of shared ownership and responsibility. However, Agile methodologies may not be suitable for all projects, particularly those with fixed requirements and tight deadlines. The lack of upfront planning and documentation can also pose challenges for teams that require a more structured and predictable process.

Traditional methodologies like the Waterfall model provide clear phases and milestones, making it easier to manage and document progress. This approach is well-suited for projects with well-defined and stable requirements, such as government contracts and regulatory compliance projects. However, the rigidity of the Waterfall model can make it difficult to accommodate changes and adapt to evolving requirements. The linear nature of the process can also result in longer development cycles and delayed feedback, increasing the risk of project failure.

Iterative and incremental methodologies, such as RUP and the Spiral model, offer a balanced approach that combines the benefits of both traditional and Agile methodologies. These methodologies provide a structured framework with defined phases and deliverables, while also allowing for continuous feedback and adaptation. The focus on risk management in the Spiral model, for example, helps identify and address potential issues early in the development process, reducing the overall risk of the project.

However, the complexity and overhead associated with these methodologies can be a challenge for smaller teams and projects with limited resources.

Lean Software Development and Kanban focus on optimizing workflow and eliminating waste, making them well-suited for projects that require a continuous flow of work and incremental improvements. The emphasis on visualizing work and limiting WIP helps teams identify bottlenecks and improve efficiency. However, the lack of prescribed roles and time-boxed iterations in Kanban can make it challenging for teams that require more structure and guidance.

In conclusion, software development methodologies provide the frameworks and processes that guide the creation of software. Each methodology offers distinct approaches to handling the complexities of software development, with its own set of principles, advantages, and challenges. The selection of an appropriate methodology depends on various factors, including the nature of the project, team size, organizational culture, and customer requirements. By understanding the strengths and limitations of each methodology, software engineers can choose the approach that best fits their needs and create high-quality software that delivers value to users and stakeholders. The continuous evolution of methodologies and the adoption of best practices from multiple approaches will continue to shape the future of software development, driving innovation and improving the effectiveness of software engineering processes.

CHAPTER 6
Software Testing and Quality Assurance

Software testing and quality assurance (QA) are critical components of the software development lifecycle. Ensuring the reliability, performance, and security of software is essential for delivering high-quality products that meet user expectations and requirements. This chapter delves into the principles, practices, and methodologies of software testing and QA, highlighting their importance in the software engineering process.

Software testing involves the systematic evaluation of software to identify defects, ensure functionality, and verify that it meets specified requirements. Testing can be conducted at various levels, including unit testing, integration testing, system testing, and acceptance testing. Each level of testing serves a specific purpose and addresses different aspects of the software.

Unit testing focuses on testing individual components or units of the software in isolation. Unit tests are typically written by developers and are designed to validate the functionality of specific code modules, classes, or functions. By isolating each unit, developers can identify and fix defects early in the development process, reducing the risk of introducing errors into the larger system. Unit testing frameworks, such as JUnit for Java, NUnit for .NET, and PyTest for Python, provide tools and libraries for writing and running unit tests.

Integration testing evaluates the interactions between integrated components or systems to ensure they work together as intended. This level of testing verifies that the interfaces and communication between different modules are functioning correctly. Integration testing can be performed incrementally, where components are tested as they are integrated, or as a "big bang," where all components are integrated and tested together. Tools like Selenium, TestNG, and JUnit can be used for integration testing, enabling automated tests to be executed across different components.

System testing involves testing the complete and integrated software system to ensure it meets the specified requirements. This level of testing validates the software's overall functionality, performance, and behavior under various conditions. System testing includes functional testing, which verifies that the software performs its intended functions, and non-functional testing, which evaluates aspects such as performance, scalability, security, and usability.

Acceptance testing, also known as user acceptance testing (UAT), is conducted to determine whether the software meets the acceptance criteria and is ready for deployment. Acceptance tests are typically performed by end-users or stakeholders and focus on validating the software's usability, functionality, and compliance with business requirements. Acceptance testing ensures that the software meets the needs of the users and aligns with their expectations.

Quality assurance (QA) encompasses the entire process of ensuring that software meets quality standards and is free from defects. QA activities include process improvement, defect prevention, and quality control. QA is a proactive approach that aims to improve the development process and prevent defects from occurring in the first place.

Process improvement involves analyzing and refining the software development process to enhance efficiency, consistency, and quality. Techniques such as process mapping, root cause analysis, and process benchmarking help identify areas for improvement and implement best practices. Process improvement initiatives, such as Capability Maturity Model Integration (CMMI) and Six Sigma, provide frameworks for achieving higher levels of process maturity and quality.

Defect prevention focuses on identifying and addressing potential sources of defects before they occur. Techniques such as code reviews, pair programming, and static code analysis help detect and eliminate defects early in the development process. Code reviews involve systematically examining code to identify errors, ensure adherence to coding standards, and improve code quality. Pair programming, where two developers work together on the same code, promotes knowledge sharing, collaboration, and early defect detection.

Quality control (QC) involves the actual testing and inspection of software to identify and correct defects. QC activities include various types of testing, such as functional testing, regression testing, performance testing, and security testing. Automated testing tools, such as Selenium, JUnit, and LoadRunner, enable the efficient execution of tests and the generation of test reports.

Functional testing verifies that the software performs its intended functions and produces the expected results. This type of testing includes techniques such as equivalence partitioning, boundary value analysis, and decision table testing. Equivalence partitioning divides input data into equivalent classes and tests representative values from each class. Boundary value analysis focuses on testing the boundaries of input ranges, where defects are more likely to occur. Decision table testing uses tables to represent combinations of inputs and their expected outputs, ensuring comprehensive coverage of different scenarios.

Regression testing ensures that changes or updates to the software do not introduce new defects or negatively impact existing functionality. Regression tests are executed after code modifications, bug fixes, or enhancements to verify that the software continues to function correctly. Automated regression testing tools, such as Selenium and JUnit, facilitate the efficient execution of regression tests and help maintain software stability.

Performance testing evaluates the software's performance under various conditions, such as different loads, stress levels, and usage patterns. Performance testing includes load testing, stress testing, and endurance testing. Load testing measures the software's ability to handle expected user loads and identifies performance bottlenecks. Stress testing evaluates the software's behavior under extreme conditions, such as high traffic or resource limitations. Endurance testing assesses the software's performance over an extended period to identify memory leaks and resource depletion.

Security testing assesses the software's vulnerability to security threats and ensures that it meets security requirements. Security testing includes techniques such as penetration testing, vulnerability scanning, and code analysis. Penetration testing simulates real-world attacks to identify potential security weaknesses. Vulnerability scanning uses automated tools to detect known vulnerabilities in the software. Code analysis examines the source code for security vulnerabilities, such as buffer overflows, injection attacks, and insecure coding practices.

Usability testing evaluates the software's user interface and user experience (UI/UX) to ensure that it is intuitive, accessible, and user-friendly. Usability testing involves observing users as they interact with the software, collecting feedback, and identifying areas for improvement. Techniques such as heuristic evaluation, cognitive walkthroughs, and user surveys help assess the software's usability and make necessary adjustments to enhance the user experience.

In conclusion, software testing and quality assurance are essential practices for delivering high-quality software that meets user expectations and requirements. By implementing systematic testing processes and quality assurance activities, software engineers can identify and address defects early in the development lifecycle, ensuring the reliability, performance, and security of the software. Understanding the principles, methodologies, and best practices of software testing and QA is crucial for building robust, efficient, and user-friendly software systems.

CHAPTER 7
Software Maintenance and Evolution

Software maintenance and evolution are integral aspects of the software development lifecycle, ensuring that software systems remain functional, efficient, and relevant over time. Maintenance involves modifying and updating software after its initial deployment to correct defects, improve performance, and adapt to changing requirements. Evolution refers to the continuous enhancement and expansion of software to meet new needs and leverage emerging technologies. This chapter explores the principles, practices, and challenges of software maintenance and evolution, highlighting their importance in sustaining the value of software systems.

Software maintenance can be categorized into four main types: corrective, adaptive, perfective, and preventive. Corrective maintenance involves identifying and fixing defects or bugs in the software. These defects may arise from coding errors, design flaws, or unexpected interactions with other systems. Corrective maintenance ensures that the software continues to function correctly and meets its intended purpose. Adaptive maintenance involves modifying the software to accommodate changes in the environment, such as hardware upgrades, operating system updates, or changes in external systems. Adaptive maintenance ensures that the software remains compatible with its environment and can continue to operate effectively. Perfective maintenance involves enhancing the software to improve performance, usability, or functionality. This may include optimizing algorithms, refining the user interface, or adding new features. Perfective maintenance aims to increase the value and satisfaction provided by the software to its users. Preventive maintenance involves making proactive changes to the software to prevent future defects or performance issues. This may include refactoring code, updating libraries, or conducting code reviews. Preventive maintenance aims to improve the software's overall quality and reduce the likelihood of future problems.

Software evolution involves the continuous enhancement and expansion of software systems to meet new needs and leverage emerging technologies. Evolution is driven by factors such as changing user requirements, technological advancements, and business needs. Software evolution can take various forms, including the addition of new features, integration with new technologies, and migration to new platforms.

The addition of new features is a common aspect of software evolution. As user needs and business requirements change, software systems must evolve to provide new capabilities and functionalities. This may involve extending existing features, developing new modules, or integrating with third-party services. The addition of new features requires careful planning, design, and testing to ensure that the changes do not introduce new defects or negatively impact existing functionality.

Integration with new technologies is another important aspect of software evolution. As new technologies emerge, software systems must evolve to leverage their benefits and remain competitive. This may involve adopting new frameworks, programming languages, or development tools. Integration with new technologies can improve the software's performance, scalability, and maintainability. However, it also presents challenges, such as ensuring compatibility with existing systems and managing the transition process.

Migration to new platforms is a significant aspect of software evolution, particularly in the context of cloud computing and mobile applications. Software systems may need to be migrated from on-premises infrastructure to cloud platforms, enabling greater scalability, flexibility, and cost-efficiency. Similarly, desktop applications may need to be migrated to mobile platforms to meet the growing demand for mobile access. Migration involves careful planning, data migration, and testing to ensure a smooth transition and minimal disruption to users.

The process of software maintenance and evolution involves several key practices and techniques. Configuration management is the process of systematically controlling changes to the software's configuration, ensuring consistency and traceability. Configuration management involves maintaining version control, tracking changes, and managing dependencies. Tools such as Git, Subversion, and Mercurial provide version control and configuration management capabilities. Change management involves managing and documenting changes to the software, ensuring that they are reviewed, approved, and implemented in a controlled manner. Change management processes, such as change requests, impact analysis, and change approvals, help ensure that changes are well-justified and do not introduce new risks or defects. Refactoring is the process of restructuring existing code to improve its readability, maintainability, and performance without changing its external behavior. Refactoring techniques, such as extracting methods, renaming variables, and removing duplicate code, help improve the quality of the codebase and make it easier to understand and modify. Regression testing ensures that changes to the software do not introduce new defects or negatively impact existing functionality. Regression tests are executed after code modifications to verify that the software continues to function correctly. Automated regression testing tools, such as Selenium and JUnit, facilitate the efficient execution of regression tests and help maintain software stability. Documentation is essential for maintaining and evolving software systems. Documentation includes design documents, user manuals, and code comments. Comprehensive and up-to-date documentation helps developers understand the software's architecture, design decisions, and implementation details, making it easier to modify and enhance the software.

Software maintenance and evolution present several challenges, including managing technical debt, ensuring backward compatibility, and maintaining quality. Technical debt refers to the accumulated cost of shortcuts, compromises, and suboptimal solutions in the codebase. Technical debt can result from rushed development, inadequate documentation, or lack of refactoring. Managing technical debt involves regularly assessing the codebase, prioritizing refactoring efforts, and allocating resources to address debt incrementally. Ensuring backward compatibility involves making changes to the software without breaking existing functionality or disrupting users. This may involve maintaining compatibility with previous versions of APIs, data formats, and protocols. Ensuring backward compatibility requires careful planning, thorough testing, and clear communication with users. Maintaining quality involves ensuring that the software continues to meet quality standards and user expectations as it evolves. This requires ongoing testing, code reviews, and quality assurance activities. Maintaining quality also involves addressing user feedback and continuously improving the software based on user needs and preferences.

In conclusion, software maintenance and evolution are critical aspects of the software development lifecycle, ensuring that software systems remain functional, efficient, and relevant over time. Maintenance involves modifying and updating software to correct defects, improve performance, and adapt to changing requirements. Evolution involves the continuous enhancement and expansion of software to meet new needs and leverage emerging technologies. By implementing systematic maintenance and evolution practices, software engineers can sustain the value of software systems and ensure their long-term success. Understanding the principles, practices, and challenges of software maintenance and evolution is essential for building and maintaining high-quality software that delivers lasting value to users and stakeholders.

CHAPTER 8
The Role of Project Management in Software Engineering

Project management is a critical component of software engineering, providing the framework and processes needed to plan, execute, and deliver software projects successfully. Effective project management ensures that software projects are completed on time, within budget, and meet the specified requirements. This chapter explores the principles, practices, and methodologies of project management in the context of software engineering, highlighting their importance in achieving project success.

Project management involves several key phases, including initiation, planning, execution, monitoring and controlling, and closing. Each phase plays a crucial role in guiding the project from inception to completion.

The initiation phase involves defining the project objectives, scope, and stakeholders. This phase includes activities such as developing a project charter, identifying key stakeholders, and establishing the project's goals and deliverables. The project charter is a formal document that outlines the project's purpose, objectives, scope, and constraints. It serves as a reference point for decision-making and provides a clear framework for the project's execution.

The planning phase involves developing a detailed project plan that outlines the tasks, resources, schedule, and budget required to achieve the project objectives. This phase includes activities such as defining the project scope, creating a work breakdown structure (WBS), estimating the effort and duration of tasks, and developing a project schedule. The project scope defines the boundaries of the project, specifying what is included and what is excluded. The WBS breaks down the project into smaller, manageable components, allowing for more precise planning and control. Estimating the effort and duration of tasks involves assessing the resources and time required to complete each task. Developing a project schedule involves sequencing the tasks, assigning resources, and determining the critical path, which is the longest sequence of tasks that must be completed on time for the project to be completed on schedule. The planning phase also includes developing a risk management plan, which identifies potential risks, assesses their impact, and outlines strategies for mitigating and managing them.

The execution phase involves carrying out the tasks and activities defined in the project plan to produce the project's deliverables. This phase includes activities such as coordinating resources, managing team members, and ensuring that tasks are completed according to the schedule and quality standards. Effective communication and collaboration are essential during the execution phase to ensure that team members are aligned and working towards the same goals. Project managers play a key role in facilitating communication, resolving conflicts, and providing support and guidance to the team.

The monitoring and controlling phase involve tracking the project's progress, measuring performance, and making adjustments as needed to ensure that the project stays on track. This phase includes activities such as monitoring task completion, tracking resource utilization, and comparing actual performance against the project plan. Key performance indicators (KPIs) and project metrics, such as schedule variance, cost variance, and earned value, provide insights into the project's performance and help identify areas for improvement. Project managers use tools and techniques such as Gantt charts, burn-down charts, and dashboards to visualize progress and make data-driven decisions. The monitoring and controlling phase also involve managing changes to the project scope, schedule, and budget. Change management processes, such as change requests, impact analysis, and change approvals, ensure that changes are evaluated and implemented in a controlled manner.

The closing phase involves finalizing all project activities, delivering the completed product to the customer, and formally closing the project. This phase includes activities such as conducting a project review, documenting lessons learned, and obtaining formal acceptance of the deliverables. The project review involves assessing the project's performance, identifying successes and areas for improvement, and capturing lessons learned for future projects. Documenting lessons learned helps build organizational knowledge and improve future project management practices. Obtaining formal acceptance of the deliverables ensures that the customer is satisfied with the product and that all contractual obligations have been met.

Several project management methodologies provide structured approaches to managing software projects, each with its principles, practices, and tools. Waterfall project management follows a linear and sequential approach, with distinct phases such as requirements gathering, design, implementation, testing, and deployment. The Waterfall methodology provides clear milestones and deliverables at each stage, making it easier to manage and document the progress of the project. However, its rigidity and lack of flexibility can be significant drawbacks, particularly for projects with evolving requirements.

Agile project management, which includes methodologies such as Scrum, Kanban, and Extreme Programming (XP), emphasizes iterative development, customer collaboration, and flexibility. Agile methodologies prioritize delivering small, incremental improvements through short development cycles, known as sprints or iterations. This approach allows teams to gather feedback early and often, adapt to changing requirements, and deliver value to customers more quickly. Agile project management involves key practices such as daily stand-up meetings, sprint planning, sprint review, and sprint retrospective meetings, which foster transparency, inspection, and adaptation.

Lean project management, inspired by Lean manufacturing principles, focuses on delivering value to customers and eliminating waste. Lean principles, such as value stream mapping, just-in-time delivery, and continuous improvement, guide the development process. Lean practices, such as limiting work in progress (WIP), visualizing workflow, and fostering a culture of learning, aim to create a more efficient and effective development process.

DevOps, a cultural and technical movement that emphasizes collaboration, automation, and continuous delivery, integrates project management practices with development and operations activities. DevOps practices, such as continuous integration, continuous delivery (CI/CD), infrastructure as code (IaC), and automated testing, streamline the development and deployment process. DevOps project management involves coordinating development and operations teams, managing infrastructure changes, and ensuring that software is delivered quickly and reliably.

Risk management is a critical aspect of project management, involving the identification, assessment, and mitigation of potential risks that could impact the project's success. Risk management processes include activities such as risk identification, risk assessment, risk mitigation planning, and risk monitoring. Identifying risks involves brainstorming potential issues, conducting risk assessments, and analyzing historical data. Assessing risks involves evaluating their likelihood and impact, using techniques such as qualitative and quantitative risk analysis. Mitigating risks involves developing strategies to reduce their likelihood or impact, such as implementing contingency plans, allocating resources, and conducting regular risk reviews. Monitoring risks involves tracking identified risks, reassessing their status, and implementing risk response actions as needed.

Effective communication is essential for successful project management, ensuring that stakeholders are informed, engaged, and aligned with the project's goals. Communication plans outline the communication needs of the project, including the frequency, format, and channels of communication. Regular status meetings, progress reports, and stakeholder updates provide transparency and keep everyone informed. Project managers play a key role in facilitating communication, addressing concerns, and ensuring that information flows smoothly between team members and stakeholders.

Team management involves leading and motivating the project team, ensuring that team members have the necessary skills, resources, and support to complete their tasks. Building a cohesive and high-performing team involves activities such as team building, conflict resolution, and performance management. Team building activities, such as workshops, training sessions, and social events, help build trust, collaboration, and a sense of shared purpose. Conflict resolution techniques, such as mediation, negotiation, and active listening, help address and resolve conflicts constructively. Performance management involves setting clear expectations, providing regular feedback, and recognizing and rewarding achievements.

In conclusion, project management is a critical component of software engineering, providing the framework and processes needed to plan, execute, and deliver software projects successfully. Effective project management ensures that software projects are completed on time, within budget, and meet the specified requirements. By understanding the principles, practices, and methodologies of project management, software engineers can achieve project success and deliver high-quality software that meets user expectations and requirements. The continuous evolution of project management practices and the adoption of best practices from multiple approaches will continue to shape the future of software development, driving innovation and improving the effectiveness of software engineering processes.

CHAPTER 9
Collaboration in Software Engineering

Collaboration is a cornerstone of software engineering, enabling teams to work together effectively to create high-quality software. Effective collaboration fosters communication, knowledge sharing, and innovation, allowing teams to leverage diverse skills and perspectives. This chapter explores the principles, practices, and tools that facilitate collaboration in software engineering, highlighting their importance in achieving project success.

Collaboration in software engineering involves several key principles, including communication, transparency, trust, and shared responsibility. These principles create a foundation for effective teamwork and drive successful outcomes.

Communication is essential for ensuring that team members are aligned, informed, and engaged. Effective communication involves clear and open channels for sharing information, ideas, and feedback. Techniques such as regular meetings, status updates, and collaborative tools help facilitate communication and ensure that everyone is on the same page.

Transparency is critical for building trust and fostering a culture of openness and accountability. Transparency involves sharing information about project progress, challenges, and decisions with the entire team. Techniques such as visual management tools, progress tracking, and open documentation help create a transparent environment where team members feel informed and involved.

Trust is the foundation of effective collaboration, enabling team members to rely on each other and work together confidently. Building trust involves creating an environment where team members feel valued, respected, and supported. Techniques such as team-building activities, regular feedback, and recognition help build and maintain trust within the team.

Shared responsibility involves recognizing that the success of the project depends on the collective efforts of the entire team. Shared responsibility means that all team members take ownership of their tasks, collaborate to solve problems, and support each other in achieving project goals. Techniques such as cross-functional teams, collective decision-making, and peer reviews help foster a sense of shared responsibility and accountability.

Several collaborative practices and methodologies enhance teamwork and drive successful outcomes in software engineering. Agile methodologies, such as Scrum and Kanban, emphasize collaboration and communication as core principles. Scrum involves regular meetings, such as daily stand-ups, sprint planning, sprint review, and sprint retrospective, to facilitate communication and collaboration. Kanban uses visual management tools, such as Kanban boards, to visualize work and promote transparency. Both methodologies encourage cross-functional teams and collective ownership of tasks.

Pair programming, a practice from Extreme Programming (XP), involves two developers working together at the same workstation, with one writing code and the other reviewing it. Pair programming promotes knowledge sharing, improves code quality, and enhances problem-solving. By working closely together, developers can identify and address issues early, share best practices, and learn from each other.

Code reviews are another collaborative practice that involves systematically examining code to identify defects, ensure adherence to coding standards, and improve code quality. Code reviews provide an opportunity for team members to share knowledge, provide feedback, and ensure consistency in the codebase. Techniques such as formal inspections, peer reviews, and automated code review tools help facilitate effective code reviews.

Collaborative tools and platforms play a crucial role in enabling teamwork and communication in software engineering. Version control systems, such as Git, Subversion, and Mercurial, provide a platform for managing code changes, tracking revisions, and facilitating collaboration among team members. Version control systems enable multiple developers to work on the same codebase, manage conflicts, and ensure that changes are tracked and documented.

Integrated development environments (IDEs), such as Visual Studio, IntelliJ IDEA, and Eclipse, provide tools and features that support collaboration, such as code editors, debuggers, and project management tools. IDEs enable developers to work efficiently, share code, and collaborate on projects.

Project management and issue tracking tools, such as Jira, Trello, and Asana, provide a platform for planning, tracking, and managing tasks and issues. These tools enable teams to visualize work, track progress, and manage dependencies. Features such as task boards, timelines, and dashboards help teams stay organized and informed.

Communication and collaboration platforms, such as Slack, Microsoft Teams, and Zoom, provide channels for real-time communication, video conferencing, and collaboration. These platforms enable team members to communicate, share files, and collaborate on tasks, regardless of their location.

Continuous integration and continuous delivery (CI/CD) tools, such as Jenkins, Travis CI, and CircleCI, automate the build, testing, and deployment processes, facilitating collaboration and ensuring that code changes are integrated and tested regularly. CI/CD tools enable teams to deliver high-quality software quickly and reliably.

Collaboration is not without its challenges, and effective teamwork requires addressing and overcoming these obstacles. Communication barriers, such as language differences, time zone differences, and remote work, can hinder collaboration. Techniques such as clear communication guidelines, regular meetings, and asynchronous communication tools help address these barriers.

Conflicts and disagreements are natural in collaborative environments, and effective conflict resolution techniques are essential for maintaining a positive and productive team dynamic. Techniques such as active listening, mediation, and compromise help resolve conflicts constructively and ensure that all team members feel heard and valued.

Balancing individual work and team collaboration can be challenging, and it's important to create an environment where both are valued and supported. Techniques such as setting clear expectations, providing flexibility, and encouraging autonomy help balance individual work and collaboration.

Building and maintaining a cohesive and high-performing team requires continuous effort and attention. Techniques such as team-building activities, regular feedback, and recognition help build trust, foster collaboration, and maintain a positive team dynamic.

In conclusion, collaboration is a cornerstone of software engineering, enabling teams to work together effectively to create high-quality software. Effective collaboration fosters communication, knowledge sharing, and innovation, allowing teams to leverage diverse skills and perspectives. By understanding the principles, practices, and tools that facilitate collaboration, software engineers can achieve project success and deliver high-quality software that meets user expectations and requirements. The continuous evolution of collaborative practices and the adoption of best practices from multiple approaches will continue to shape the future of software development, driving innovation and improving the effectiveness of software engineering processes.

CHAPTER 10
Software Security and Ethical Hacking

Software security is a critical aspect of software engineering, aimed at protecting applications, data, and systems from unauthorized access, threats, and vulnerabilities. As software becomes increasingly interconnected and pervasive, the need for robust security measures has never been greater. This chapter explores the principles of software security, common threats, best practices, and the role of ethical hacking in safeguarding software systems.

Security threats come in various forms, including malware, phishing attacks, denial-of-service (DoS) attacks, and data breaches. Malware, short for malicious software, includes viruses, worms, and ransomware that can disrupt operations, steal information, or hold systems hostage. Phishing attacks trick users into divulging sensitive information by masquerading as trustworthy entities. DoS attacks overwhelm systems with traffic, rendering them unavailable to legitimate users. Data breaches involve unauthorized access to sensitive data, often resulting in significant financial and reputational damage.

To mitigate these threats, software engineers must adopt a proactive approach to security, incorporating best practices and security principles throughout the development lifecycle. The foundational principles of software security include confidentiality, integrity, availability, authentication, and authorization.

Confidentiality ensures that sensitive information is only accessible to authorized users. This principle is achieved through encryption, access controls, and secure communication protocols. For example, data transmitted over networks should be encrypted using protocols like TLS (Transport Layer Security) to prevent eavesdropping and interception. Access controls, such as role-based access control (RBAC), restrict access to sensitive data based on user roles and permissions.

Integrity ensures that data is accurate and has not been tampered with. Techniques such as hashing and digital signatures help verify the integrity of data. Hash functions generate a fixed-length hash value for a given input, making it easy to detect changes to the data. Digital signatures, created using asymmetric encryption algorithms, provide a way to verify the authenticity and integrity of data.

Availability ensures that systems and data are accessible to authorized users when needed. Redundancy, fault tolerance, and disaster recovery plans help maintain availability in the face of hardware failures, network outages, and other disruptions. For example, load balancing distributes traffic across multiple servers, ensuring that no single server becomes a bottleneck or point of failure.

Authentication verifies the identity of users and processes, while authorization determines their access rights and privileges. Implementing multi-factor authentication (MFA) and strong password policies enhances the security of authentication mechanisms. MFA requires users to provide multiple forms of verification, such as a password and a one-time code sent to their mobile device, making it more difficult for attackers to gain unauthorized access.

Secure coding practices are essential for writing code that is resistant to common security vulnerabilities. Input validation, proper error handling, and avoiding the use of hardcoded credentials are key practices for preventing security issues. Tools such as static code analyzers and security testing frameworks can help identify and address security issues early in the development process. For example, input validation ensures that user-provided data is checked for correctness and sanitized to prevent injection attacks, such as SQL injection and cross-site scripting (XSS).

Encryption is a key technique for protecting sensitive data, both at rest and in transit. By encrypting data, software engineers can ensure that it remains confidential and secure, even if it is intercepted or accessed by unauthorized parties. Implementing strong encryption algorithms and key management practices is essential for maintaining data security. For example, symmetric encryption algorithms, such as AES (Advanced Encryption Standard), are used for encrypting large amounts of data, while asymmetric encryption algorithms, such as RSA (Rivest-Shamir-Adleman), are used for secure key exchange and digital signatures.

Ethical hacking, also known as penetration testing, involves simulating attacks on software and systems to identify and address security weaknesses. Ethical hackers use the same techniques as malicious attackers but do so with the goal of improving security. Penetration testing helps organizations uncover vulnerabilities before they can be exploited by malicious actors, enabling them to take corrective actions. Ethical hackers follow a structured approach, which includes reconnaissance, vulnerability scanning, exploitation, and post-exploitation analysis.

Security testing is an integral part of the software development lifecycle. It includes various types of testing, such as vulnerability scanning, security code reviews, and penetration testing. Automated security testing tools, such as OWASP ZAP and Burp Suite, can help identify vulnerabilities and provide actionable insights for remediation. Vulnerability scanning involves using automated tools to scan applications for known security issues, such as outdated software versions, misconfigurations, and weak passwords. Security code reviews involve manually inspecting code for security vulnerabilities, such as insecure coding practices and logic flaws.

Incident response and recovery are critical components of a comprehensive security strategy. Organizations must have plans and procedures in place to detect, respond to, and recover from security incidents. This includes monitoring for security breaches, conducting forensic analysis, and implementing measures to prevent future incidents. Incident response plans typically include steps for identifying and containing the incident, eradicating the threat, recovering affected systems, and communicating with stakeholders.

The role of security in DevOps, known as DevSecOps, emphasizes integrating security into the DevOps process. DevSecOps practices involve automating security testing, continuous monitoring, and incorporating security checks into CI/CD pipelines. This approach ensures that security is an integral part of the development lifecycle, rather than an afterthought. For example, security checks can be integrated into the CI/CD pipeline to automatically scan code for vulnerabilities, enforce security policies, and verify compliance with security standards.

In the evolving landscape of cybersecurity, it's important to stay ahead of emerging threats. New types of attacks and vulnerabilities are constantly being discovered, requiring continuous learning and adaptation. Threat intelligence services provide valuable information about the latest threats, helping organizations anticipate and defend against potential attacks. Machine learning and AI are also being used to enhance threat detection and response, analyzing patterns and anomalies to identify suspicious activities.

Cybersecurity frameworks and standards, such as ISO/IEC 27001, NIST Cybersecurity Framework, and GDPR, provide guidelines and best practices for implementing and managing security. Compliance with these standards helps organizations ensure that their security measures are comprehensive and effective. Regular audits and assessments are essential for maintaining compliance and identifying areas for improvement.

Security awareness training is crucial for educating employees about cybersecurity risks and best practices. Human error is often a significant factor in security breaches, so it's important to train employees to recognize phishing attempts, use strong passwords, and follow security policies. Regular training sessions, simulated phishing attacks, and awareness campaigns can help reinforce good security habits.

In conclusion, software security and ethical hacking are essential practices for protecting applications, data, and systems from threats and vulnerabilities. By adopting a proactive approach to security, incorporating best practices, and conducting regular security testing, software engineers can build robust and secure software that withstands the challenges of today's digital landscape. The integration of security into the software development lifecycle, through practices such as DevSecOps, further strengthens the security posture of organizations, ensuring that security is built into every stage of the development process. As the threat landscape continues to evolve, staying informed about emerging threats, leveraging advanced technologies, and fostering a culture of security awareness will be critical for safeguarding software systems.

CHAPTER 11
The Future of Software Engineering

The future of software engineering is shaped by rapid advancements in technology and evolving industry trends. Emerging technologies, such as artificial intelligence (AI), blockchain, and quantum computing, are poised to transform the way software is developed, deployed, and maintained. This chapter explores these cutting-edge technologies, their potential impact on software engineering, and the trends that are likely to shape the future of the industry.

AI and machine learning are already having a profound impact on software engineering, and their influence is expected to grow. AI-driven tools and platforms are automating various aspects of software development, from code generation and bug detection to performance optimization and user experience enhancement. As AI technologies continue to advance, they will enable more intelligent and adaptive software systems, capable of learning and evolving over time.

One of the most promising applications of AI in software engineering is automated code generation. AI models, trained on vast repositories of code, can generate code snippets, functions, or even entire applications based on high-level specifications. This capability can significantly speed up development processes, reduce the likelihood of errors, and enable developers to focus on higher-level design and problem-solving tasks. For example, AI-powered tools like GitHub Copilot can suggest code completions and generate boilerplate code, improving developer productivity.

Another area where AI is making a significant impact is in bug detection and resolution. Machine learning models can analyze code patterns and historical data to identify potential bugs and suggest fixes. These models can also prioritize issues based on their severity and likelihood of occurrence, helping developers address critical problems more efficiently. Automated bug detection tools can continuously monitor code repositories and alert developers to potential issues, enabling proactive maintenance and reducing the risk of software failures.

Performance optimization is another domain where AI is proving invaluable. AI-driven tools can analyze application performance metrics, identify bottlenecks, and suggest optimizations. For instance, machine learning algorithms can predict the impact of code changes on performance, allowing developers to make informed decisions about optimizations. Additionally, AI can be used to automatically tune application configurations, ensuring optimal performance under varying workloads and conditions.

User experience (UX) enhancement is also benefiting from AI technologies. AI models can analyze user behavior and preferences to provide personalized experiences and recommendations. For example, recommendation engines, powered by machine learning algorithms, can suggest relevant content, products, or features based on user interactions. AI-driven UX tools can also optimize interface layouts, improve accessibility, and enhance usability, creating more engaging and user-friendly applications.

Blockchain technology is another transformative force in software engineering. By providing a decentralized and secure way to record transactions and manage data, blockchain has the potential to revolutionize industries such as finance, supply chain, and healthcare. Software engineers are exploring ways to integrate blockchain into applications, enabling new levels of transparency, security, and trust.

One of the key benefits of blockchain technology is its ability to create immutable and tamper-proof records. This makes it ideal for applications that require secure and transparent transaction tracking, such as supply chain management, digital identity verification, and financial services. Blockchain can also enable smart contracts, which are self-executing contracts with the terms of the agreement directly written into code. Smart contracts can automate and enforce complex business processes, reducing the need for intermediaries and minimizing the risk of fraud.

Quantum computing represents a paradigm shift in computing, with the potential to solve complex problems that are currently intractable for classical computers. Quantum algorithms, such as Shor's algorithm for factoring and Grover's algorithm for search, promise to revolutionize fields like cryptography, optimization, and drug discovery. As quantum hardware and software mature, software engineers will need to develop new skills and approaches to harness the power of quantum computing.

Quantum computing leverages the principles of quantum mechanics, such as superposition and entanglement, to perform computations that are beyond the capabilities of classical computers. This enables quantum computers to solve certain types of problems exponentially faster than classical computers. For example, Shor's algorithm can factor large integers in polynomial time, breaking widely used cryptographic schemes like RSA. Grover's algorithm can search unsorted databases with a quadratic speedup, offering significant advantages for optimization and search problems.

The rise of edge computing is reshaping the way software is deployed and managed. Edge computing involves processing data closer to the source, reducing latency and improving performance for applications that require real-time processing. This trend is driving the development of new software architectures and deployment models, enabling more efficient and responsive systems.

Edge computing is particularly relevant for applications that generate large volumes of data, such as IoT devices, autonomous vehicles, and industrial automation systems. By processing data at the edge, near the source of data generation, organizations can reduce the need for data transmission to centralized data centers, minimizing latency and bandwidth usage. This enables faster decision-making and more responsive applications, enhancing the overall user experience.

The increasing importance of data privacy and security is also shaping the future of software engineering. With regulations like the General Data Protection Regulation (GDPR) and the California Consumer Privacy Act (CCPA) enforcing stricter data protection requirements, software engineers must prioritize privacy and security in their designs. Techniques such as differential privacy, homomorphic encryption, and secure multi-party computation are becoming more relevant as organizations seek to protect sensitive data while enabling data-driven innovation.

Differential privacy is a technique that allows organizations to analyze and share aggregate data while protecting the privacy of individual data points. Homomorphic encryption enables computations to be performed on encrypted data without decrypting it, ensuring data privacy during processing. Secure multi-party computation allows multiple parties to jointly compute a function over their inputs while keeping those inputs private. These techniques provide powerful tools for maintaining data privacy and security in an increasingly data-driven world.

The future of software engineering will also be influenced by advancements in human-computer interaction (HCI) and user interface (UI) design. Emerging technologies, such as augmented reality (AR), virtual reality (VR), and natural language processing (NLP), are enabling more intuitive and immersive user experiences. Software engineers will need to design interfaces that leverage these technologies to create engaging and user-friendly applications.

In conclusion, the future of software engineering is marked by continuous innovation and adaptation. Emerging technologies and evolving industry trends are driving new opportunities and challenges, requiring software engineers to stay abreast of advancements and continuously expand their skill sets. By embracing change and leveraging cutting-edge technologies, software engineers can shape the future of software and drive positive impact across industries. The integration of AI, blockchain, quantum computing, edge computing, and advanced privacy techniques will redefine the boundaries of what is possible, ushering in a new era of intelligent, secure, and resilient software systems.

TOBI MAKINDE

CHAPTER 12
The Intersection of Software and Hardware

The intersection of software and hardware is a dynamic and evolving landscape that plays a crucial role in the development of modern technology. Understanding the relationship between software and hardware is essential for building efficient, reliable, and high-performance systems. This chapter explores the intricate interplay between software and hardware, examining various layers of abstraction, key technologies, and emerging trends.

Software interacts with hardware through various layers of abstraction, including operating systems, device drivers, and firmware. The operating system (OS) serves as an intermediary between software applications and hardware components, managing resources such as memory, CPU, and input/output (I/O) devices. Device drivers are specialized software that enable the OS to communicate with hardware peripherals, such as printers, graphics cards, and network adapters. Firmware, which is embedded in hardware devices, provides low-level control and functionality.

Operating systems play a pivotal role in managing hardware resources and providing a stable environment for software applications. They handle tasks such as process scheduling, memory management, file system operations, and device communication. Popular operating systems, such as Windows, macOS, and Linux, offer a range of features and capabilities tailored to different types of hardware and user requirements. For example, real-time operating systems (RTOS) are designed for applications that require precise timing and low-latency responses, such as industrial automation and embedded systems.

Embedded systems are a prime example of the close interplay between software and hardware. These systems consist of specialized hardware and software designed to perform specific functions within larger systems. Examples include automotive control systems, medical devices, industrial automation, and consumer electronics. Developing embedded systems requires a deep understanding of both hardware and software, as well as the ability to optimize performance and resource utilization.

One key challenge in embedded systems development is managing the limited resources available on the hardware platform. Embedded devices often have constrained processing power, memory, and storage, requiring efficient software design and optimization techniques. For instance, real-time operating systems (RTOS) are used in embedded systems to provide deterministic behavior and meet strict timing requirements. RTOS manage task scheduling, interrupt handling, and resource allocation to ensure that critical tasks are executed within specified time constraints.

The Internet of Things (IoT) represents another area where software and hardware intersect. IoT devices, such as smart home appliances, wearable sensors, and connected vehicles, rely on a combination of hardware sensors, microcontrollers, and software applications to collect, process, and transmit data. Software engineers working on IoT projects must consider factors such as power consumption, connectivity, security, and interoperability to ensure the seamless integration of devices within the IoT ecosystem.

IoT devices often operate in resource-constrained environments, requiring efficient power management and communication protocols. Low-power wireless communication technologies, such as Bluetooth Low Energy (BLE), Zigbee, and LoRa, enable IoT devices to transmit data while minimizing energy consumption. Additionally, IoT platforms and frameworks, such as AWS IoT, Microsoft Azure IoT, and Google Cloud IoT, provide tools and services for device management, data analytics, and application development.

Hardware acceleration is a technique used to enhance the performance of software applications by offloading specific tasks to dedicated hardware components. Graphics processing units (GPUs) are commonly used for hardware acceleration in graphics rendering, scientific computing, and machine learning. Field-programmable gate arrays (FPGAs) and application-specific integrated circuits (ASICs) are also used to accelerate tasks such as encryption, network processing, and data compression. Leveraging hardware acceleration requires software engineers to write code that can efficiently utilize these specialized hardware resources.

GPUs, originally designed for rendering graphics, have become essential for accelerating parallel computations in various domains. Their ability to perform thousands of simultaneous operations makes them ideal for tasks such as deep learning, image processing, and scientific simulations. Software frameworks like CUDA and OpenCL provide APIs for programming GPUs, enabling developers to harness their computational power for general-purpose applications.

FPGAs are configurable hardware devices that can be programmed to perform specific tasks with high efficiency. Unlike general-purpose processors, FPGAs can be reconfigured to optimize performance for particular workloads. This flexibility makes them valuable for applications that require low-latency processing, such as real-time data analytics, financial trading, and network security. High-level synthesis tools and languages, such as VHDL and Verilog, are used to design and implement FPGA-based solutions.

Virtualization and cloud computing have further blurred the lines between software and hardware. Virtualization technology allows multiple virtual machines (VMs) to run on a single physical server, abstracting the underlying hardware and enabling more efficient resource utilization. Cloud computing platforms, such as Amazon

Web Services (AWS), Microsoft Azure, and Google Cloud, provide virtualized infrastructure and services, allowing software engineers to deploy and scale applications without managing physical hardware. Understanding virtualization and cloud computing is essential for building scalable, flexible, and cost-effective software solutions.

Virtualization technology enables organizations to consolidate hardware resources, reduce costs, and improve operational efficiency. Hypervisors, such as VMware ESXi, Microsoft Hyper-V, and KVM, manage the creation and execution of virtual machines, providing isolation and resource allocation. Containers, such as Docker, offer lightweight virtualization by packaging applications and their dependencies into portable units, ensuring consistency across different environments.

Cloud computing platforms provide a wide range of services, including infrastructure as a service (IaaS), platform as a service (PaaS), and software as a service (SaaS). IaaS offerings, such as Amazon EC2 and Google Compute Engine, provide virtualized compute resources, allowing organizations to scale their infrastructure on demand. PaaS offerings, such as Microsoft Azure App Service and Google App Engine, provide development and deployment environments, abstracting the underlying infrastructure and enabling rapid application development. SaaS offerings, such as Salesforce and Office 365, deliver software applications over the internet, reducing the need for on-premises installations and maintenance.

The integration of software and hardware is also driving advancements in fields such as robotics, autonomous systems, and augmented reality (AR). Robots and autonomous systems rely on a combination of sensors, actuators, and software algorithms to perceive their environment, make decisions, and perform tasks. AR applications overlay digital information onto the physical world, requiring precise synchronization between software, hardware, and user interfaces.

Robotics applications, such as autonomous vehicles, drones, and industrial robots, require sophisticated software algorithms for navigation, perception, and control. Sensor fusion techniques combine data from multiple sensors, such as cameras, lidar, and radar, to create accurate representations of the environment. Machine learning algorithms, such as deep reinforcement learning, enable robots to learn and adapt to complex tasks. Middleware frameworks, such as the Robot Operating System (ROS), provide tools and libraries for developing and integrating robotic applications.

AR applications, such as Microsoft HoloLens and Google ARCore, enhance user experiences by blending digital content with the physical world. These applications require real-time processing of sensor data, accurate tracking of user movements, and rendering of virtual objects. AR software development kits (SDKs) provide tools and APIs for building AR applications, enabling developers to create immersive and interactive experiences.

In conclusion, the intersection of software and hardware is a critical aspect of modern technology development. Understanding the interplay between these two domains is essential for building efficient, reliable, and high-performance systems. By leveraging the strengths of both software and hardware, engineers can create innovative solutions that drive progress across a wide range of industries. The continuous advancements in operating systems, embedded systems, IoT, hardware acceleration, virtualization, and emerging technologies such as robotics and AR will continue to shape the future of software engineering, enabling new possibilities and transforming the way we interact with technology.

CHAPTER 13
Open-Source Software and Community Development

Open-source software (OSS) has become a driving force in the software industry, enabling collaboration, innovation, and the democratization of technology. Open-source projects are developed and maintained by communities of contributors who share their code, knowledge, and expertise, fostering a culture of transparency and collective improvement. This chapter explores the principles of open-source software, its benefits, challenges, and the role of community development in driving technological advancements.

The open-source movement began in the late 20th century as a response to the proprietary software model, which restricted access to source code and limited the ability to modify and distribute software. The Free Software Foundation (FSF), founded by Richard Stallman in 1985, and the Open-Source Initiative (OSI), established in 1998, played pivotal roles in promoting the principles of open source and free software. These organizations advocate for software freedom, emphasizing the rights to use, study, modify, and distribute software.

Open-source licenses, such as the GNU General Public License (GPL), the MIT License, and the Apache License, provide legal frameworks that define the terms under which software can be used, modified, and distributed. These licenses ensure that open-source software remains free and accessible, while also protecting the rights of contributors and users. For example, the GPL requires that any modified versions of the software be released under the same license, ensuring that improvements are shared with the community. The MIT and Apache licenses are more permissive, allowing for greater flexibility in how the software can be used and integrated into proprietary projects.

One of the most significant advantages of open-source software is its collaborative development model. Open-source projects benefit from the collective contributions of developers, testers, and users from around the world. This diverse pool of talent and perspectives leads to more robust, secure, and innovative software. Collaborative development also fosters a sense of community and shared ownership, as contributors work together towards common goals.

Popular open-source projects, such as the Linux operating system, the Apache web server, and the Mozilla Firefox browser, have demonstrated the power of open-source development. These projects have achieved widespread adoption and success, thanks to the contributions of dedicated communities. The Linux kernel, for example, is developed by thousands of contributors and is used in a wide range of applications, from servers and supercomputers to smartphones and embedded systems. The Apache HTTP Server is the most widely used web server software, powering millions of websites and applications. Mozilla Firefox, an open-source web browser, has played a significant role in promoting web standards and user privacy.

Open-source software also provides significant benefits for organizations and businesses. By leveraging open-source solutions, companies can reduce development costs, accelerate time-to-market, and avoid vendor lock-in. Open-source software is often more secure and reliable than proprietary alternatives, as it undergoes continuous scrutiny and improvement by the community. Additionally, the use of open-source software promotes interoperability and standardization, facilitating integration and collaboration across different systems and platforms.

For example, many organizations use open-source content management systems (CMS) like WordPress and Drupal to build and manage their websites. These platforms offer a wide range of plugins and themes, allowing businesses to customize their websites to meet specific needs. Open-source databases, such as MySQL and PostgreSQL, are widely used for data storage and management, providing reliable and scalable solutions for various applications. Open-source development frameworks, such as Django and Ruby on Rails, enable rapid application development and deployment, reducing the time and effort required to bring new products to market.

Contributing to open-source projects offers numerous opportunities for professional growth and development. Developers can gain valuable experience, enhance their skills, and build a portfolio of work that showcases their expertise. Participation in open-source communities also provides networking opportunities, enabling developers to connect with peers, mentors, and potential employers. For many developers, contributing to open source is a way to give back to the community and make a positive impact on the world.

Open-source development is not without its challenges. Managing and coordinating contributions from diverse and distributed teams can be complex and time-consuming. Ensuring code quality, security, and compliance with licensing requirements requires diligent oversight. Maintaining a sustainable project also involves securing funding, managing infrastructure, and providing support to users and contributors. Despite these challenges, the open-source model has proven to be a resilient and effective approach to software development.

Community development plays a crucial role in the success of open-source projects. Strong communities provide the support, resources, and collaboration needed to drive innovation and sustain long-term development. Community development involves engaging with contributors, fostering a welcoming and inclusive environment, and promoting the project's goals and values.

Effective communication and collaboration tools are essential for managing open-source projects. Version control systems, such as Git, provide a platform for tracking changes, managing contributions, and coordinating work. Issue trackers, such as GitHub Issues and JIRA, help manage tasks, track progress, and prioritize work. Communication platforms, such as mailing lists, forums, and chat applications, enable real-time collaboration and knowledge sharing.

Open-source foundations and organizations, such as the Apache Software Foundation, the Linux Foundation, and the Eclipse Foundation, provide governance, funding, and support for open-source projects. These organizations help ensure the sustainability and growth of open-source initiatives by providing resources, infrastructure, and advocacy.

In conclusion, open-source software and community development have transformed the software industry, enabling collaboration, innovation, and the democratization of technology. By embracing the principles of openness, transparency, and collective improvement, open-source communities continue to drive progress and create software that benefits everyone. For software engineers, participating in open-source projects offers valuable opportunities for learning, growth, and making a positive impact on the world. The ongoing success of open-source projects demonstrates the power of community-driven development and the potential for open-source software to shape the future of technology.

CHAPTER 14
The Business of Software Engineering

The business of software engineering involves more than just writing code. It encompasses the entire lifecycle of software development, from ideation and design to development, deployment, and maintenance. Understanding the business aspects of software engineering is essential for building successful software products and services that meet the needs of users and generate value for stakeholders. This chapter explores the key considerations, strategies, and best practices for building and sustaining a successful software engineering business.

One of the key considerations in the business of software engineering is identifying and understanding the target market. This involves conducting market research to identify user needs, preferences, and pain points. By understanding the market, software engineers can design and develop solutions that address real-world problems and provide value to users. Market research also helps in identifying potential competitors and understanding the competitive landscape.

Market research involves gathering and analyzing data from various sources, such as surveys, interviews, focus groups, and industry reports. This data provides insights into user demographics, behaviors, and preferences, helping software engineers tailor their products to meet specific needs. For example, a company developing a project management tool might conduct surveys to understand the features and functionalities that users find most valuable, enabling them to prioritize development efforts accordingly.

Monetizing software involves selecting the right business model for the product or service. There are various business models to consider, including:

1. Licensing: Selling licenses for the software, allowing users to install and use it on their devices. Licensing can be perpetual (one-time payment) or subscription-based (recurring payments). Perpetual licenses provide a one-time revenue boost, while subscription models offer a steady stream of recurring revenue. Licensing is commonly used for enterprise software, where organizations purchase licenses for multiple users.

2. Software as a Service (SaaS): Offering software as a subscription service, where users access the software through a web browser or app. SaaS provides ongoing revenue and allows for continuous updates and improvements. SaaS models are popular for cloud-based applications, such as customer relationship management (CRM) systems, collaboration tools, and online storage services.

3. Freemium: Providing a basic version of the software for free, with the option to purchase premium features or services. This model allows users to try the software before committing to a purchase. Freemium models are effective for attracting a large user base and converting free users into paying customers. Examples of freemium software include productivity apps, communication tools, and entertainment platforms.

4. Advertising: Generating revenue through advertisements displayed within the software. This model is common in free-to-use applications and platforms. Advertising revenue is driven by user engagement and traffic, making it important to attract and retain a large user base. Advertising is commonly used in social media platforms, content websites, and mobile apps.

5. Open Source: Offering the software for free under an open-source license, while generating revenue through related services such as support, consulting, and custom development. Open-source business models leverage the community-driven nature of open-source software to build a user base and create opportunities for monetization through value-added services.

Selecting the right business model depends on various factors, including the nature of the software, the target market, and the revenue goals. It is also important to consider scalability, as the chosen model should support growth and expansion.

Marketing and promotion are critical components of the business of software engineering. Effective marketing strategies help raise awareness, attract users, and generate interest in the software. This can include digital marketing, social media campaigns, content marketing, search engine optimization (SEO), and public relations. Building a strong brand and establishing a positive reputation are essential for long-term success.

Digital marketing involves using online channels to reach and engage with potential customers. Social media platforms, such as Facebook, Twitter, and LinkedIn, provide opportunities for targeted advertising and community building. Content marketing involves creating valuable and informative content, such as blog posts, whitepapers, and videos, to attract and educate potential users. SEO focuses on optimizing the software's online presence to improve search engine rankings and drive organic traffic.

Customer support and engagement are also vital for maintaining user satisfaction and loyalty. Providing timely and effective support helps address user issues and enhances the overall user experience. Engaging with users through feedback, surveys, and community forums provides valuable insights into user needs and preferences, enabling continuous improvement and innovation.

In addition to these business aspects, software engineers must also navigate legal and regulatory considerations. This includes ensuring compliance with data protection and privacy laws, intellectual property rights, and industry-specific regulations. Understanding the legal landscape and seeking legal counsel, when necessary, helps mitigate risks and protect the business.

Data protection and privacy regulations, such as the General Data Protection Regulation (GDPR) and the California Consumer Privacy Act (CCPA), impose strict requirements on how organizations collect, store, and process personal data. Compliance with these regulations involves implementing data protection measures, obtaining user consent, and providing transparency about data practices. Intellectual property rights, such as copyrights, trademarks, and patents, protect the software and its components from unauthorized use and infringement.

Successful software engineering businesses also focus on building strong, collaborative teams. This involves hiring skilled and motivated professionals, fostering a positive and inclusive work culture, and providing opportunities for professional growth and development. Effective leadership, clear communication, and a shared vision are essential for driving innovation and achieving business goals.

Building a strong team starts with attracting and retaining top talent. This involves offering competitive compensation, creating a supportive and inclusive work environment, and providing opportunities for career advancement. Professional development programs, such as training workshops, mentorship, and continuous learning opportunities, help employees stay updated with the latest technologies and best practices.

Effective project management is also crucial for the success of software engineering businesses. This involves planning, executing, and monitoring projects to ensure they are completed on time, within budget, and to the required quality standards. Agile methodologies, such as Scrum and Kanban, provide frameworks for managing projects in a flexible and iterative manner, enabling teams to respond to changing requirements and deliver value to users.

In conclusion, the business of software engineering involves a holistic approach that encompasses market research, business model selection, marketing, customer support, legal considerations, and team building. By understanding and addressing these aspects, software engineers can build successful software products and services that meet user needs and generate value for stakeholders. The ability to navigate the business landscape is a crucial skill for software engineers who aspire to create impactful and sustainable software solutions. By adopting best practices, leveraging innovative technologies, and fostering a collaborative and inclusive work culture, software engineering businesses can thrive in a competitive and rapidly evolving industry.

CHAPTER 15
Building a Career in Software Engineering

Building a successful career in software engineering requires a combination of technical skills, continuous learning, and professional development. The field of software engineering is dynamic and constantly evolving, offering numerous opportunities for growth and advancement. This chapter explores the key steps and strategies for building a rewarding and impactful career in software engineering.

One of the foundational skills for a career in software engineering is proficiency in programming languages. Understanding the syntax, semantics, and best practices of languages such as Python, Java, C++, JavaScript, and others is essential for writing effective and efficient code. Developing expertise in multiple languages and paradigms, such as object-oriented, functional, and procedural programming, broadens a software engineer's skill set and enhances their problem-solving abilities.

In addition to programming languages, software engineers must also be familiar with software development tools and frameworks. Integrated development environments (IDEs), version control systems, build tools, and testing frameworks are essential for efficient and collaborative development. Familiarity with popular frameworks and libraries, such as React, Angular, Django, and Spring, is also important for building modern applications.

Continuous learning is a crucial aspect of a successful software engineering career. The rapid pace of technological advancements means that software engineers must stay updated with the latest trends, tools, and practices. This can be achieved through various means, such as online courses, workshops, conferences, reading technical blogs and articles, and participating in coding challenges and hackathons. Joining professional organizations and communities, such as the Association for Computing Machinery (ACM) or the IEEE Computer Society, provides access to valuable resources and networking opportunities.

Building a strong portfolio is an effective way to showcase skills and experience to potential employers or clients. A portfolio can include personal projects, contributions to open-source projects, and professional work. Documenting projects with detailed descriptions, code samples, and demonstrations helps highlight technical expertise and problem-solving capabilities. For example, a portfolio might include a web application developed using React and Node.js, with detailed explanations of the design, implementation, and challenges encountered.

Networking and building professional relationships are also important for career growth. Attending industry events, joining online forums and communities, and participating in local meetups provide opportunities to connect with peers, mentors, and potential employers. Building a professional online presence, such as maintaining a LinkedIn profile and contributing to platforms like GitHub and Stack Overflow, enhances visibility and credibility in the field.

Soft skills, such as communication, teamwork, and problem-solving, are equally important for a successful career in software engineering. Effective communication skills enable software engineers to convey ideas clearly, collaborate with team members, and interact with stakeholders. Teamwork skills are essential for working in cross-functional teams and contributing to collective goals. Problem-solving skills help software engineers tackle complex challenges and develop innovative solutions.

Career advancement in software engineering can take various paths, including technical specialization, management, or entrepreneurship. Technical specialists, such as software architects, DevOps engineers, and data scientists, focus on deepening their expertise in specific areas. Management roles, such as project managers, team leads, and CTOs, involve overseeing projects, teams, and strategic initiatives. Entrepreneurship offers the opportunity to start and grow a software business, leveraging technical skills and business acumen.

Certifications and advanced degrees can also enhance career prospects. Certifications from reputable organizations, such as AWS, Microsoft, and Google, validate technical skills and knowledge. Pursuing advanced degrees, such as a Master's or Ph.D. in Computer Science or Software Engineering, provides deeper insights into specialized areas and opens up opportunities for research and academic careers.

Certifications demonstrate a commitment to professional development and expertise in specific technologies or practices. For example, AWS Certified Solutions Architect and Microsoft Certified: Azure Solutions Architect Expert certifications validate skills in cloud architecture and services. Certified ScrumMaster (CSM) and Project Management Professional (PMP) certifications validate skills in project management and Agile methodologies. These certifications can enhance job prospects and open doors to new opportunities.

Pursuing advanced degrees provides opportunities for deeper learning and specialization. Master's programs in computer science or software engineering often include coursework in advanced topics, such as machine learning, cybersecurity, and software architecture. Ph.D. programs offer opportunities for research and innovation, contributing to the advancement of knowledge in the field. Advanced degrees can also lead to academic and research careers, enabling software engineers to teach, mentor, and conduct cutting-edge research.

Mentorship is a valuable aspect of professional development. Finding a mentor who can provide guidance, support, and advice can help navigate the complexities of a software engineering career. Mentors can share their experiences, provide feedback on projects, and offer insights into industry trends and best practices. Mentorship relationships can be formal or informal, and can be established through networking, professional organizations, or workplace programs.

In conclusion, building a career in software engineering involves a combination of technical skills, continuous learning, professional development, networking, and soft skills. By staying updated with the latest trends, building a strong portfolio, and actively participating in the professional community, software engineers can achieve success and make a meaningful impact in the field. The dynamic and evolving nature of software engineering offers numerous opportunities for growth, advancement, and innovation. Whether pursuing technical specialization, management, or entrepreneurship, software engineers can build rewarding and impactful careers by embracing continuous learning, fostering professional relationships, and staying adaptable to the changing landscape of technology.

CHAPTER 16
The Impact of Emerging Technologies on Software Engineering

The landscape of software engineering is continually evolving, shaped by the emergence of new technologies that challenge conventional practices and open up unprecedented possibilities. These emerging technologies, such as blockchain, quantum computing, and edge computing, are transforming the way software is designed, developed, and deployed. Understanding their impact is crucial for software engineers who seek to stay at the forefront of innovation and harness these advancements to create cutting-edge solutions.

Blockchain technology, known for its decentralized and secure nature, has introduced new paradigms in data management and transaction processing. Originally popularized by cryptocurrencies like Bitcoin, blockchain's potential extends far beyond digital currencies. In software engineering, blockchain offers robust solutions for enhancing security, transparency, and trust in various applications. For instance, in supply chain management, blockchain can provide a transparent and immutable ledger of transactions, ensuring traceability and reducing fraud. Similarly, in the healthcare industry, blockchain can securely manage patient records, providing access control while maintaining data integrity. The integration of blockchain into software systems requires engineers to adopt new development methodologies and tools, focusing on decentralized application (DApp) development, smart contracts, and consensus algorithms.

Quantum computing, leveraging the principles of quantum mechanics, promises to revolutionize problem-solving capabilities in software engineering. Unlike classical computers that use bits as the smallest unit of information, quantum computers use quantum bits or qubits, which can represent and process multiple states simultaneously. This quantum parallelism enables quantum computers to solve complex problems exponentially faster than classical computers. For software engineers, this means developing algorithms and applications that can leverage quantum computing's power to tackle previously intractable problems. Quantum algorithms, such as Shor's algorithm for factorizing large numbers and Grover's algorithm for searching unsorted databases, demonstrate the potential of quantum computing in cryptography and data analysis. However, quantum computing is still in its nascent stage, and software engineers must stay abreast of advancements in quantum programming languages, quantum development frameworks, and the evolving hardware landscape.

Edge computing represents another significant shift in software engineering, emphasizing the processing of data closer to the source rather than relying on centralized cloud servers. This approach reduces latency, improves response times, and enhances the efficiency of data-intensive applications. Edge computing is particularly relevant in the context of the Internet of Things (IoT), where a vast number of devices generate massive amounts of data that require real-time processing. For instance, autonomous vehicles rely on edge computing to process sensor data and make split-second decisions. Similarly, in industrial automation, edge computing enables predictive maintenance and real-time monitoring of equipment. Software engineers must design and develop applications that can operate efficiently in distributed environments, addressing challenges related to data synchronization, security, and resource management.

Artificial intelligence (AI) and machine learning (ML) are also profoundly impacting software engineering, driving innovation across various domains. AI and ML technologies enable software systems to learn from data, adapt to changing conditions, and make intelligent decisions. In software development, AI-driven tools and platforms are automating tasks such as code generation, bug detection, and performance optimization. For example, AI-powered code completion tools like GitHub Copilot can suggest entire code snippets based on the developer's intent, significantly boosting productivity. ML algorithms are being integrated into software applications to provide personalized user experiences, predictive analytics, and autonomous decision-making capabilities. Software engineers must acquire skills in AI and ML, understanding concepts like neural networks, reinforcement learning, and natural language processing, to effectively harness these technologies.

The rise of 5G technology is also transforming software engineering by providing ultra-fast, low-latency communication networks. 5G enables the development of applications that require real-time data transmission and high bandwidth, such as augmented reality (AR), virtual reality (VR), and advanced IoT solutions. For software engineers, 5G opens up new possibilities for creating immersive and interactive experiences. AR and VR applications, which require high data transfer rates and minimal latency, can benefit from 5G's capabilities, providing users with seamless and realistic experiences. In smart cities, 5G can support a wide range of IoT devices, enabling efficient traffic management, energy distribution, and public safety services. Developing software for 5G networks requires engineers to optimize their applications for high-speed data transfer, network slicing, and edge computing integration.

In conclusion, emerging technologies are reshaping the landscape of software engineering, introducing new paradigms, methodologies, and opportunities. Blockchain, quantum computing, edge computing, AI, ML, and 5G are just a few of the technologies driving this transformation. For software engineers, staying at the forefront of these advancements is essential to leveraging their potential and creating innovative solutions that address complex challenges. By embracing these technologies and continuously updating their skills, software engineers can play a pivotal role in shaping the future of technology and driving progress across various industries.

CHAPTER 17
Future Trends in Software Engineering

As we look toward the future, the field of software engineering is poised for continued transformation, driven by emerging trends and evolving technologies. These future trends will not only shape the way software is developed and deployed but also redefine the skills and practices required of software engineers. Understanding these trends is crucial for professionals who aim to remain competitive and innovative in a rapidly changing landscape.

One of the most significant future trends in software engineering is the increasing emphasis on artificial intelligence (AI) and machine learning (ML). As AI and ML technologies mature, their integration into software development processes will become more pervasive. AI-driven tools will further automate various aspects of software engineering, from code generation and testing to project management and decision-making. Software engineers will need to develop expertise in AI and ML algorithms, frameworks, and tools to harness their full potential. Additionally, ethical considerations surrounding AI, such as bias, transparency, and accountability, will become increasingly important, requiring engineers to adopt responsible AI practices.

The rise of low-code and no-code platforms is another trend set to revolutionize software engineering. These platforms enable users with little or no coding experience to create applications through visual interfaces and pre-built components. By democratizing software development, low-code and no-code platforms empower business users and domain experts to participate in the development process, accelerating the delivery of solutions and reducing the burden on traditional software developers. However, this trend also presents challenges, such as ensuring the scalability, security, and maintainability of applications built on these platforms. Software engineers will need to adapt by focusing on integrating low-code solutions with existing systems, providing governance, and ensuring compliance with best practices.

The concept of DevSecOps is gaining traction as security becomes an integral part of the software development lifecycle. DevSecOps extends the principles of DevOps by embedding security practices into every stage of development, from design and coding to testing and deployment. This approach addresses the growing need for secure software in an era of increasing cyber threats and data breaches. Software engineers will need to acquire skills in secure coding practices, automated security testing, and threat modeling to effectively implement DevSecOps. Additionally, collaboration between development, security, and operations teams will be essential to fostering a culture of security and ensuring the delivery of robust and secure software.

Quantum computing is expected to become a mainstream technology, bringing with it the need for new programming paradigms and approaches. While still in its early stages, quantum computing promises to solve complex problems that are currently beyond the reach of classical computers. As quantum hardware and software continue to advance, software engineers will need to familiarize themselves with quantum algorithms, quantum programming languages, and quantum development frameworks. The integration of quantum computing into existing systems and workflows will require innovative solutions to bridge the gap between classical and quantum computing environments.

Sustainability and green software engineering are emerging as important considerations in the development of software systems. As concerns about climate change and environmental impact grow, software engineers are increasingly focusing on creating energy-efficient and sustainable software. This involves optimizing algorithms for lower energy consumption, designing software that can run on energy-efficient hardware, and adopting practices that reduce the carbon footprint of software development and deployment. Green software engineering also encompasses the use of renewable energy sources for data centers and cloud services, as well as promoting sustainable practices across the entire software lifecycle.

The proliferation of the Internet of Things (IoT) will continue to drive innovation in software engineering. With billions of connected devices generating vast amounts of data, software engineers will need to develop applications that can handle real-time data processing, analytics, and decision-making. IoT solutions will require robust security measures to protect against cyber threats and ensure data privacy. Additionally, the integration of IoT with AI and edge computing will enable the development of intelligent and autonomous systems, transforming industries such as healthcare, agriculture, and manufacturing.

In the realm of user experience (UX) design, there is a growing emphasis on creating more intuitive, accessible, and inclusive software. As software becomes an integral part of everyday life, the need for user-friendly and accessible applications is paramount. Software engineers and UX designers will need to collaborate closely to create interfaces that are not only visually appealing but also easy to use and accessible to all users, including those with disabilities. The adoption of design thinking principles and user-centered design practices will be crucial in achieving these goals.

Another future trend in software engineering is the increasing use of augmented reality (AR) and virtual reality (VR) technologies. AR and VR are transforming the way users interact with software, providing immersive and interactive experiences. These technologies are finding applications in various fields, including gaming, education, healthcare, and retail. Software engineers will need to develop skills in AR and VR development, understanding the unique challenges and opportunities these technologies present. This includes optimizing performance, ensuring realistic rendering, and creating intuitive user interfaces in virtual environments.

In conclusion, the future of software engineering is shaped by emerging trends and evolving technologies that present both opportunities and challenges. AI and ML, low-code and no-code platforms, DevSecOps, quantum computing, sustainability, IoT, UX design, and AR/VR are just a few of the trends that will influence the field in the coming years. For software engineers, staying informed and adaptable is essential to leveraging these trends and driving innovation. By continuously updating their skills and embracing new technologies and methodologies, software engineers can play a pivotal role in shaping the future of software development and delivering solutions that address the complex challenges of a rapidly changing world.

www.ingramcontent.com/pod-product-compliance
Lightning Source LLC
LaVergne TN
LVHW092007090526
838202LV00001B/44